Real People,
Real Past Lives

Real People, Real Past Lives

DAVID WELLS

HAY HOUSE

Australia • Canada • Hong Kong • India
South Africa • United Kingdom • United States

First published and distributed in the United Kingdom by:
Hay House UK Ltd, 292B Kensal Rd, London W10 5BE. Tel.: (44) 20 8962 1230; Fax: (44) 20 8962 1239. www.hayhouse.co.uk

Published and distributed in the United States of America by:
Hay House, Inc., PO Box 5100, Carlsbad, CA 92018-5100. Tel.: (1) 760 431 7695 or (800) 654 5126; Fax: (1) 760 431 6948 or (800) 650 5115. www.hayhouse.com

Published and distributed in Australia by:
Hay House Australia Ltd, 18/36 Ralph St, Alexandria NSW 2015. Tel.: (61) 2 9669 4299; Fax: (61) 2 9669 4144. www.hayhouse.com.au

Published and distributed in the Republic of South Africa by:
Hay House SA (Pty), Ltd, PO Box 990, Witkoppen 2068. Tel./Fax: (27) 11 467 8904. www.hayhouse.co.za

Published and distributed in India by:
Hay House Publishers India, Muskaan Complex, Plot No.3, B-2, Vasant Kunj, New Delhi – 110 070. Tel.: (91) 11 4176 1620; Fax: (91) 11 4176 1630. www.hayhouse.co.in

Distributed in Canada by:
Raincoast, 9050 Shaughnessy St, Vancouver, BC V6P 6E5. Tel.: (1) 604 323 7100; Fax: (1) 604 323 2600

A catalogue record for this book is available from the British Library.

ISBN 978-1-84850-022-8

Printed and bound by CPI Bookmarque, Croydon CR0 4TD.

This book is dedicated to my teacher, Jenni Shell,

and my twin soul, Jenny Greentree,

for their support through many of my own past lives

as well as this. Emmis.

Contents

Acknowledgements

I would like to acknowledge my friends Lee, Jarvis, Norie, Wayne, Diane and many more who supported me by staying away when I was in the throes of book fever and all those who wrote to me with their extraordinary experiences, whether they are in the book or not. My special thanks to Rachel, Cathy, Andrew, Sue, Jennie, Jill, Tessa, Mark and Matthew.

As ever, I would like to thank Hay House for their support with so much more than the book, Jo Burgess and Michelle Pilley in particular for their solid advice and practical solutions, and Lizzie Hutchins for her Libra balancing act on editing out my Gemini ramblings.

And of course to my mum and sister for being there – always.

CHAPTER 1

PAST-LIFE REGRESSION: THE THEORIES

Is it true?

What do you think? You have picked up a book that's clearly about past lives, the past lives of people like you and me, ordinary folk going about their daily business but with a tale to tell that may sound a little odd to some – or not. Perhaps you will recognize something that has happened to you among these words – I hope so!

You may have been drawn to this book because you have already had a past-life experience, maybe through a dream or a feeling of familiarity when you have been visiting another place. What this book shows is that anyone can have an experience at any time. The stories here have come from all sorts of people – those on a spiritual path, those who are just starting on one and those who have never even considered such a thing but are now that little bit more interested. But one thing is for sure: past-life experiences always leave people changed and often lead them to consider the possibility of reincarnation.

A Question of Faith

The idea of reincarnation isn't a new-age thing, a term that makes me laugh anyway, as the thought of anything here being new is ludicrous. It's all ancient – the only thing that's new is the transfer of information through books, DVDs, movies, etc. And that's great, because it's quicker than travelling to your local shaman to hear what's occurring!

The belief that we have a soul is actually as old as Methuselah, and he was no spring chicken, but what came first – our soul or our belief in it? There's a thought...

Whatever the answer, many older cultures actively encourage the idea of the soul travelling through a series of lives. Take the Jewish faith, which even has a word for it, Gilgul, and references to it are found in the Kabbalah; and of course Aborigines believe in it, as do Buddhists. And what self-respecting Druid doesn't think their soul goes on forever?

Some faiths do believe that one soul, one incarnation, is the general rule of thumb, and that may be so, but why go to all the trouble of forming interpersonal relationships and dealing with life's trials and tribulations and celebrations only to do it once? In astrological terms, why bother waiting for a particular planetary line-up if you're only here once? Astrology, too, includes the likelihood of reincarnation and there's more on past-life astrology at the back of the book, as well as a chance to discover more about your own reasons for incarnating this time around.

We all have our own belief systems and it's finding what sits best with you that's important. Personally, I am all for structure in the way we learn about our soul's journey, as it gives an etiquette to proceedings rather than making it just a random pick and mix, but I believe that permissive rather than authoritative structures work best, as ultimately your own creativity is what makes this journey special for you.

Ultimately, you have to judge for yourself whether past lives are true or not. It's my very strong belief that any proof has to be a personal one; my truth isn't yours and yours cannot be mine. But I hope you will want to look further into the mirror that is your own soul to see what it reflects back to you – literally!

Communicating with your Soul

Your soul holds the chip that fits into your personal navigation system. It knows when to turn right, when to turn left and when to stop, but of course you switch it off, change your mind, don't listen and on occasions talk over it and miss your turning. Past-life work can help you reconnect to that part of yourself that wants to guide you and if you do it often enough it becomes a way to enhance your own psychic ability as well. Imagine finding a life where you were a psychic, an oracle or a seer. Bringing back some of those tools could help you immeasurably on your spiritual journey.

Other reasons to visit a past life could include:

- learning about yourself and why you do or want to do certain things
- gaining a better perspective on a relationship
- realizing where a habit comes from and learning how to stop it
- rediscovering and building on a skill
- finding the root of a phobia and beginning to deal with it.

Some people in this book are out of time and place; they feel drawn to a bygone era. Some are well versed in today's systems and ways of being but can hear the call of their soul reminding them that they have been here before and that some information from a previous time could be of use to them. Maybe you feel the same and are ready to hurry up and find it, but how do you do that?

You have three layers: your conscious self, your subconscious self and your higher spiritual self – personality, soul and spirit. By getting all three to work together you can read the messages that are meant to flow up and down. Some of you will be very conscious, personality-led, some will be very subconscious, soul-led, and some will be perhaps a little too heavenly minded, and of course that means spiritually led, which may sound lovely but remember we live on Earth, so practical stuff has to be done!

Connecting all three selves is the task of your past-life therapist, or you if you're doing this on your own. Get it right and you will harvest your past-life memories and use them not only to advance your development by listening to your soul but also to bring resolution to your personality and peace to your world. The route you take is up to you, but remember you don't have to be on a spiritual path, the direct descendant of a medium or the seventh son of a seventh son, you just need to be you. That's more than enough to find these lives. They're your lives, after all, and this is your journey.

Teachers Old and New

Much of what you learn will come from those around you, those who have taken on the role of teacher, and you in turn will be their guru, even if sometimes reluctantly! Think about who teaches you the most. Could the person who breezes in, upsets the apple cart and breezes back out again teach you more than the one who sits by your side agreeing with everything you say? It's not always as clear as you might think.

Soul links come in all shapes and sizes. Just as you can fall in love with someone in five minutes or over a lifetime, so you can recognize someone's soul instantly or it can take a past-life regression to remind you of just what you have been through together over the centuries, what lessons you have taught each other and which of those you may no longer want to carry on with!

I knew when I got pregnant with my son that I was expecting a boy. My son and I both know that we have known each other before and that I was only with my first husband to have him. I believe that there is some link between my past family and my ex-husband's past family and we had to get together to

allow my son to have this link. He can re-
member past lives and I can remember that
in one of my past lives I drowned on a ship.

Lynn

If you feel you have a link with someone, investigate it further. And don't worry about the relationships you had in the past. Some people think it strange that their kids were their husbands and their mothers their uncles, but so what? It's all about different lives, different relationships and different times. It's about learning from each other, and learning is why we are here, is it not?

Some people look to past-life regression to uncover the truth of reincarnation, while others want to see what the experience can give them and how it can help here and now. For most it's a combination, but whatever you get from a regression, you can rest assured it will be of value to you if you take the time to think about it.

CHAPTER 2

QUESTIONS AND ANSWERS

I am asked questions all the time, and not just about past-life regression – but that's a good thing! There is nothing wrong with questions. Blind faith is no faith at all; you should always be asking questions. I drove my teacher bonkers asking questions, but it's what we're here for. So here are a few questions – and answers – about past-life regression.

IS IT REAL OR MY IMAGINATION?

I attended your workshop at the mind, body and spirit event a few weeks ago (which I really enjoyed, by the way). I bought your book and decided to go through the guided meditation again and I got some stuff and dates which I checked on the Internet and they all fitted together.

I know you probably get asked this all the time, but how do you know if what you are seeing is from a past life and is not just an overactive imagination at work?

At your workshop I got something very odd which I don't think can even exist, so I would be very interested to know if there is any way of deciding what might be a past life and what might be imagination.

Debs

Debs answers her own question here when she says, 'I got some stuff and dates which I have checked on the Internet and they all fitted together,' but I guess her next question could be: 'Have I seen them before in a book or in a movie?'

When I am carrying out regressions I often have clients say mid-regression that they think they are seeing something they have seen before. When this happens I ask them very quickly to save the evaluations for later and just go with what they see during their visualization.

Often it's an emotional response that proves to people that they are really seeing past lives. If you're telling a story, you don't get emotionally involved; if you're telling a story about your life, you can get over-emotional, and that can and does happen with past-life regression.

Michele wrote to me about her experience:

Apparently I've been here many times and come back just for the fun of it. I guess that's just me. I know of three of my past lives and am bursting with curiosity about one in particular.

The first one was not so long ago, during the Second World War. I was a little girl of about seven and I had a baby brother and both parents. My dad was at home but wore a suit and tie – make of that what you will. I passed with a horrible illness. During regression, I was in bed, having difficulty breathing and coughing up black stuff. As I passed into spirit I could hear sobbing. It was very distressing.

An earlier life was during the crusades. I was a young man and I can remember feeling terribly angry at what was happening around me. I passed due to a sword entering at the base of my spine and exiting through my chest. Apparently that is the origin of my spinal stenosis in this life.

The one I am bursting with curiosity about is from the time of Henry VIII. In 1982 I was watching television with my family when the Mary Rose *was being raised from the seabed in Portsmouth. Inexplicably, I became hysterical. I was screaming at the TV, saying, 'They can't bring it up!' My family sat and stared – well, you would. When the ship was dropped back into the sea, I started to laugh. I wasn't watching the second time they brought her up. I've no idea why I reacted in such a way, but I have had messages from Henry and even saw him once when I was eight or nine and he just said, 'You.' I must admit I'm a little afraid to find out what that was all about, but I'm sure I will one day.*

Although we don't know how Michele was regressed, there are some valuable questions begging to be answered here. Why indeed did she react that way on seeing the *Mary Rose* resurrected? It's interesting how something as seemingly mundane as watching television can spark a past-life memory, but the subconscious never forgets, it records everything you have ever done and when there's a trigger, the memories come flooding back. Don't discount these brief peeps through the window of time. Ask what they could be...

ARE OUR PAST LIVES ABLE TO BRING ILLNESS INTO THIS?

Another question arising from Michele's experience is whether an injury from a past life could carry itself with such severity into this one.

I understand the theory that when we leave one life we aren't so different in the next, but there must be more to it than that. This is an interesting area that I have yet to explore and would like to do so when time and energy permit. I know that birthmarks can show themselves on the sites of past-life injuries, as I have two on my own body – one on my back where a knife went in and one on my ankle where an arrow went through my leg.

I have also heard stories of people who have this ache or that pain and when they have a regression it magically goes away, but I have yet to see any evidence of it. That doesn't mean to say it can't happen – even I can be surprised now and again! However, I am very firmly of the school of thought that says medicine first, so if you are suffering from a mysterious ailment, go to a doctor, not a past-life therapist!

CAN YOU GET STUCK WHEN YOU VISIT YOUR PAST LIVES?

This is something else that people can worry about, but 'no' is the short answer to this one. The worst than could happen is that you nod off and miss the whole thing, but you can't get stuck, your personality is far too noisy to let that happen. You may hear all sorts of stories about people having regressions and then staying as their former characters for the rest of their lives, but these are really not likely to be true – I have never ever seen or had a report of such a thing.

WHAT IF I DON'T LIKE WHAT I SEE?

Regardless of what you see in a past life, you will only get the information you need. Sometimes it is difficult, but remember where it's coming from – from your soul, that part of you that holds all your memories and has your very best interests at heart.

If you do find yourself in a regression and you don't want to go any further, you must say so. If you're being regressed by another person, they will then bring you back out of it. If you're doing it on your own, simply open your eyes and wiggle your fingers and toes. Clap your hands maybe – anything to remind yourself you're back in the physical world.

WHAT IF I HAVE A FAMOUS LIFE?

How exciting! Maybe you can find out where you buried the treasure, but I doubt it! It's a myth that everyone was Cleopatra – of course they weren't. Those who perpetuate the myth about everyone finding out they were famous in a past life aren't usually that familiar with past-life work and its process – it's normally a very dismissive point of view, in my experience.

It's more likely you will experience an ordinary life but sometimes with extraordinary events within it, or even famous people passing through. Later we will hear from Rachel, who saw Elizabeth I in a past life but really had nothing to do with her. Elizabeth was a point of reference for the time Rachel found herself in.

Of course it would be silly to say that nobody has famous lives or lives where they were involved with famous people; whilst rare, it does happen. There's an example later in the book.

SHOULD YOU DO PAST-LIFE REGRESSION YOURSELF OR GET SOMEONE ELSE TO DO IT FOR YOU?

That's entirely up to you. You may prefer to go it alone or you may be grateful for a little support along the way. Remember, though, that it's always you who does the work; the therapist is there to guide and help you, not do it all for you. Sometimes my clients think I am doing some sort of magical thing, but they are the one creating the real magic. I do use guides and angelic forces when I set up a room, mind you...

Of course not everyone approaches past-life work on a psychic level and some people prefer to seek the professional counsel of a hypnotherapist rather than that of an intuitive. That choice, too, has to be yours and yours alone. It seems to me that the results are pretty much the same, it's really a matter of personal preference, but always remember to go on recommendation rather than take pot luck, and take someone with you, at least on your first visit. That way you're going to feel happier and that can make you more relaxed, and relaxed is what you need to be!

Also, make sure you are ready for a regression – it isn't something you should rush into. If your intuition, angels, guides or magic beans tell you it's best to leave it alone for a while, maybe you should listen.

Above all, just remember the golden rules:

- **P**ersonal recommendation.
- **A**sk as many questions as you need.
- **S**oul speaks, you follow!
- **T**ake someone with you as support.

A past-life regression should be a natural thing, a beautiful thing...

Someone who was intrigued by the subject and went to a regression therapist was Pippa Quelch. She writes:

I'm a journalist working for BBC Radio Devon, based in Plymouth. I have never been married and don't have any children, but met my soul mate about a year and a half ago. Byron runs Haunted Devon, a paranormal investigation team. We met through work – I was recording a documentary with his team and enjoyed the experience so much I joined up. Within six months we were inseparable. Although neither of us knows exactly how or why we got together, we've been told that our late grandfathers had a hand in it! We also both feel we have known each other before.

Joining the team has really opened me up in a spiritual sense. I still describe myself as an open-minded sceptic because I feel I need to retain balance as a journalist, but I would love to be able to uncover firm evidence of the paranormal and really like to offer challenging ideas and theories to my listeners. My past-life experience happened when I decided to record a regression feature for my Saturday breakfast programme and approached regression therapist Deborah Monshin (who now lives and works in Cumbria).

I experienced two supposed past lives during my regression session. Throughout the whole time I was fully aware of who I was and what I was doing, though I kept worrying that the mini-disc would stop recording! I didn't go into a deep trance, although I did imagine lots of things in my mind's eye and kept giving out that information to Deborah. I was also very aware of my personality changing as I spoke more about each past life. In the first I was timid, frightened and very lonely. In the second I was a bitter, self-important and extremely frustrated character.

Past Life 1

Deborah took me down a mental corridor and asked me to pick a door to go through. She asked me where I was and it took ages for me to focus. I could then feel I was wearing a heavy backpack and thick boots. I was wearing some kind of military uniform.

Deborah asked me to reach into my pocket and I pulled out a photograph of a young woman. When I saw it I burst into tears and realized that I would never see her again. I realized in that moment that I was a battle-

field deserter – I was a very young man who had fled from conflict.

It was bitterly cold and barren where I was and I had an overwhelming feeling of hopelessness. I didn't want to return to fighting, but couldn't go home because my family and childhood sweetheart, whom I'd hoped to marry, would be ashamed of me. I was unloved, unwanted and didn't know where to turn.

Deborah then progressed me to the next point, where I was imprisoned in some kind of military jail. I heard men speaking in a foreign language and was aware of terrible pains in my lower stomach. I was desperately hungry and had been ill treated. Later I was taken to some kind of hospital wing of the prison. There were men with terrible injuries all around me – I could see explosion wounds and blood everywhere.

I couldn't stop crying throughout the regression and kept talking of my family and wanting to be back home, secure and happy. I died in the prison, perhaps through starvation and other injuries.

When asked to look at myself lying on the bed I saw a very thin dark-haired young man, possibly called John. Interestingly, in my current life I am extremely close to my family and can't imagine being far from them.

Past Life 2

After such an emotional introduction to regression I was hoping for a nicer life when I reached the next door.

I saw the yellow brick road and immediately started laughing. It seemed such an obvious image – just like in the film when Dorothy opens the door of the farmhouse in the Land of Oz. When I realized the scene was staying with me – I could see the set, lighting and film crew – I was delighted. I thought maybe I had been Judy Garland in a past life. What a scoop! But then I could see her talking to a producer or maybe the director – and Toto the dog was weeing on one of the cardboard flowers!

I looked down at my feet and could see a pair of pixie boots. Then I realized I was one of the Munchkins. The first thing I felt was anger. I was disgusted that I had to wear thick, silly make-up and a ridiculous costume. I felt uncomfortable and hot. I hadn't even been given a speaking part. I'd wanted to be the mayor – I was a much better actor than the man who had that part. I didn't like the cast or the crew and refused to get too involved with any of them. I was a serious actor, but my physical appearance prevented me from obtaining any decent acting roles.

Through questioning from Deborah I was able to explain that I lived with my mother in some kind of trailer park. I think we had a rather poor, nomadic lifestyle. My father had been abusive and had abandoned us when I was a baby, perhaps ashamed of having a dwarf son. I idolized my mother and hoped to become rich and famous so that I could buy us a nice house and lifestyle. My sexuality was a touchy subject. I knew I would never marry – I didn't like women. When asked if I was gay, I refused to answer. I said the subject was disgusting and I didn't want to talk about it.

Deborah progressed me to the next big landmark in my life: my mother's death. I felt overwhelming loss and became extremely emotional. I knew I couldn't live without her, so later committed suicide with an overdose of pills washed down with whiskey. I got a sense that alcohol abuse was a big part of my life then – certainly not something that is reflected in my life now. I've never had drink or drug issues, so I find it interesting to have regressed to a life in which it was clearly a problem.

****

Details of the battlefield deserter were too sketchy for research, but I immediately went out and bought the DVD of The Wizard of Oz *to see if I felt any affinity with any of the Munchkin actors. I didn't seem to, though. I also searched the Internet for details of any Munchkin actor who had committed suicide – with no result. The lack of hard detail in my regressions has hampered any research attempts and most of the Munchkins have passed away now. This has frustrated me more than anything! I'm longing to know whether I truly experienced a past life or whether I was exercising my rather vivid imagination.*

My present life is relatively comfortable, successful and happy, so experiencing two lives of misery and loneliness was rather up-setting. I wonder whether I did manage to learn important lessons in my past lives and whether the progress I made then has made this life easier. The regression opened up a huge number of questions and I would love to undergo more regressions at some point.

Listeners to my programme seemed either fascinated by the subject or deeply angered that I had even considered 'dabbling' with regression. It remains a controversial subject – it's a tricky balance to hit.

It's a shame Pippa couldn't name the actor, but sometimes these details escape us and, like Pippa, we are left frustrated. The solution is of course to do exactly what she suggested herself and have another one (or two) regressions.

Although Pippa's lives weren't exactly fun, it has to be said that they have a common link, and it's *time* on this occasion. Both were very recent and they seemed to follow pretty sharply after each other. Could those two tough lives really be the reason why this one is happy, comfortable and successful? Are we given a rest now and again, a life where things aren't quite so tough? And does that mean that next time Pippa's soul will take up where it left off and misery will be back on the menu? Probably not, but I do believe some lives are designed to be that little bit easier than others. Maybe the soul sometimes wants a holiday, and who could blame it?!

Pippa also said that some of her listeners were fascinated by past lives and some were angered that she was dabbling in such things. It's been my experience that past-life regression is a very personal choice, but we live in a world where everyone thinks they have a say in what we believe or do. They don't, of course, but some people like to think they do. For me, have a regression or don't have one, I will respect your choice either way, but if you don't have one, leave me to get on with mine without criticism.

Alice Potter also got in touch with me to share some of her experiences. Alice is a hypnotherapist in – I'll let her tell you!

I am 53 years old, married, with 6 children ranging in age from 31 down to 11. I live in the north-east of England now but have travelled widely and lived in Hungary, Belgium and Egypt. As my family career seemed to be teaching, and that would fit in with having a large bunch of children of my own, I trained to be a teacher when we returned from Egypt and lived for eight years in Kent. I specialized in special needs teaching and continued with that when I moved back to the north-east. However I always felt that

I had somehow been shut in the wrong box and when the chance came up to train as a professional hypnotherapist, I grabbed it.

I have been in practice now for five years and have loved every minute of it. One of my favourite areas of work is past-life regression, though I do all the 'usual' stuff as well, such as smoking, anxiety, stress, confidence building, etc.

I'd like to tell you about Elizabeth. She called me to arrange a past-life regression session as she had had recurring dreams since she was a small child. In the dreams she was kneeling in front of a gravestone in a wind-blown graveyard that seemed to be near the top of a cliff. She always had a feeling of dread and seemed to hear the name 'Annie' being called. As she grew older she had the dream more and more often and found that she saw a little more of the area around her. She still heard the name 'Annie', but never got any more details. The feelings of dread and confusion were still there and were beginning to get her down.

About three years ago she went to visit Whitby in Yorkshire for the first time ever and was amazed to find that she seemed to recognize the place and particularly the abbey and graveyard on top of the cliffs. In fact she rushed into the graveyard and went straight to a particular gravestone, where everything began to feel just like the dream. Of course, it would have been great if the stone had said 'Annie', but it was too worn to read!

Elizabeth was convinced that this was a past life and wanted me to regress her to it so she could find out the full story behind it. Of course, even when you think you know something of a past life, your subconscious mind can take you elsewhere, and I made that clear to her before we started. [An excellent point – you can never be sure you'll get what you ask for.]

She went straight to a very vivid life where she described wearing a brown rough cloth dress or robe. She seemed to have some sort of dirty cloth or bandages on her feet and a thin leather belt with a key hanging on it which seemed really important to her. It was the key to a single-roomed stone building which seemed to have straw on the roof and was situated alone at the edge of a track which ran around some fields and led to a town in the distance. She felt she was very thin and her hands were red and sore as she was a washerwoman.

In the hut or building she seemed to be caring for an older relative that she called Jack. He seemed to go out when she was around but stay in the hut when she went to work in a big house not far away. Her name was Maggie, not Annie. In the big house she was the lowest of the low, but she developed a fancy for a young man named Charles or Charlie, who seems to have been a son of the household, and he took advantage of her belief that she was in love with him, with the usual consequences of a baby being conceived. His family would not let him marry her, although she always believed he would, and she believed he loved her.

We then moved to a time when the baby was about a year old and was coughing and coughing. There was no medicine and no money for medicine, and the child was dying. At this point Elizabeth became very upset and began calling out the baby's name: 'Annie, Annie!' She described her dying in her arms.

Then we moved on a little in time. By now Jack had also died from what seemed like a heart attack or stroke and Maggie had gone to kneel in the graveyard near the cliff. Jack and Annie were buried there as it was the nearest town and church to where Maggie lived.

The cook from the big house where Maggie worked was passing by and she came up and told her that the young man who had fathered Annie had now been safely married off by his father. Maggie suddenly despaired. Elizabeth vividly described standing up and turning towards the cliff, then running straight at it and flying off the top. At this point she began to cough and choke and make grasping movements with her hands. She described how cold the water was and how huge the rocks were around her, how she came up to the surface and was desperate because she was not dead but was then swept under again.

I helped her to let go and move above her body. She became calm eventually and was happy because she could be with Annie again and let that life go.

When I asked if there was anything she had learned from that life she wanted to tell me all about using a lace-making nee-dle and mending tears in sheets, but she did acknowledge that the young man from Maggie's life was someone she knew in this life, but he had no influence on her this time around.

Recently, Elizabeth told me that she felt as if a great weight had been lifted off her now and the feelings of loss and dread had all vanished. She intends to visit Whitby again soon and see if she can do some follow-up research for herself.

Childhood dreams can often be related to past lives, though more often than not they fade and are replaced by the stresses and strains of modern life. Elizabeth, though, met her concerns head-on and was rewarded with the feeling of completion and of recognition. A weight was lifted from her life.

Alice went on to tell me about another regression she did:

This is a regression I did myself, using self-hypnosis, which was very vivid and memorable.

I found myself in the middle of some sort of ritual. It was dark and there was aromatic smoke burning in stone stands of some sort and fires to light the place. There were lots of people around and drumming and chanting could be heard. We seemed to be in a field which was in a dip or bowl-shaped area of land. It was a very important place and felt like a church almost.

I looked down and saw that I was wearing a long straight robe which was a dark green sort of colour and some kind of twisted gold band around my forehead. The most amazing thing was I felt such power, as if I was in control of all this and I knew everything. There were some sort of stones arranged in an archway and this led into a tunnel.

It was the end of whatever ritual I had been conducting and I was leaving the tunnel to return to where I lived. I was an older woman and had been doing this since I was a child. I also had a younger woman with me who seemed to be my daughter and also my helper. As we walked to the place where we lived, a crowd followed behind in a deferential sort of way, still chanting and drumming. Just as we reached the village we were confronted by a large group of men with sticks and axes. They had long hair and wore outer clothes made of skins and furs. Their leader told us that they had all decided that my way had come to an end and they were taking over the power and were about to destroy any traces of me.

To my horror all the people around took their side, even my daughter, as if they had been waiting for this moment. My life was spared, but I was banished to live in a cave. Although food was brought to me, I was not allowed out again and even the power of magic, which I thought I could command, did not help me.

The strongest feeling I had in the cave was one of betrayal by people who I thought loved me and to whom I felt I had done no wrong, as they had seemed to trust me and believe in my power. Most keenly I felt the loss of that status and power that had been my whole life. Eventually I died of choking on something – perhaps I was poisoned? I was all alone. I regretted leaving because I still felt – even then – that a time would come when I would get my power and status back.

Coming back, I realized I had met the leader of the uprising in at least two other past lives and he had turned against me when I trusted him in those lives too.

I think I am aware of the life Alice mentions and I have come across some very similar stories from that time. When Alice is ready, I am sure she will go back to discover more.

Although I have never met her, she strikes me as being a very sincere and talented lady. Some of the power she once had has clearly come through with her into this incarnation and even though she is using hypnotherapy I am sure her intuitive gifts are very strong! If you would like to contact her yourself, her details are at the back of the book.

There are many ways to be regressed and many great people like Alice out there who can help you on your voyage of discovery. Let's look at a few more methods now.

CHAPTER 3

SIMPLE METHODS, EXTRAORDINARY RESULTS

So, how do you go about finding out about your past lives? There are many ways and means and we all work differently. There's more on how to meditate and explore past lives through several routes in my book *Past, Present and Future* (Hay House, 2007), but in this book I will focus on my own method, a method used to visit the Akashic records. Are you ready to begin?

Creative Visualization

First let's look at how you see through your inner eye:

Think about your own front door.

Have a good look at it.

Now imagine what it would be like to touch it, to feel it... Put your ear against it and listen to it creaking if you like!

Do you feel as though you're outside your own front door now?

Your imagination has the power to make you feel as if you're really standing in front of your door – or anywhere – and that is all visualization is. You see pictures as if you were in a certain place, or time, and allow information to come to you, and it will.

Soul Communication

Earlier we looked at communicating with your soul. You don't have to have a past-life regression to do this – there are many other ways. In ancient Greece labyrinths were all the rage. A labyrinth is a map on sacred ground that you can walk through to re-mind yourself of your need to reach a source. As you walk it, your mind becomes more and more focused on your true intent and less concerned with some of the earthly nonsense we have to deal with. When you reach the centre and turn and take the walk back, your soul retreats and all the nonsense returns. Perhaps those ancient cultures knew more than we think.

Another way, which may be familiar to those of you who have been to one of my seminars or workshops, is the exercise where you gaze into another person's eyes or use a mirror and gaze into your own and just look for the soul to make a link. It may show you something from a past life that way. Bear in mind if you do this as a partnership you are more likely to see the lives of your partner than your own, so give each other feedback. It's important to trust the person you are working with, too. Want to try it? Here's how:

Get a shaving mirror, or one of those rectangular mirrors similar in shape and size to a rear-view mirror in a car, or get a partner!

- Make yourself comfortable and take a deep breath. Breathing is a good thing! Breathe in and out really deeply three times.

- Now hold the mirror up so you can see your eyes – just your eyes – and let your vision go *through* the mirror. Gaze through it and soften your eyes. Alternatively, gaze into your partner's eyes and then look right through them.

- Keep gazing through the mirror/eyes and wait for any changes to your own eyes or your partner's face or any images to come into your mind. Let your soul communicate with you.

This may not sound like much, but it's very powerful. When you become more adept at it, try and ask your soul a question, for example, 'What's the right path?' Then pay attention to your own intuition.

Julie and Stewart wrote and told me what they found when they looked into each other's eyes. They are a brother and sister who both live in Sutton Coldfield and are single with no children. Julie runs her own secretarial business and has been doing so for ten years. Stewart is a trained solicitor.

When we did the exercise I looked Stewart straight in the right eye and I could see something right away, which sort of freaked me out! I saw a girl who I thought was about eight years old. The most noticeable thing about her was she had something covering her head. To me, it looked like the head covering that Plymouth Brethren women wear and I felt that she was religious, though I don't know why. I didn't really notice anything about her top, but my eye was drawn further down and she had a skirt on that was sort of shaped like a handkerchief and very specifically she had boots on that had eyelets on them. The whole thing seemed to be in grey and white. Nothing was spoken but I had the feeling that she was a very calm little girl. I also had the feeling that she lived just above the Wash near Hull – again, don't know why!

Julie

When I looked into my sister's right eye I did as David asked and let my eyes relax and after 20 or so seconds I had the image of an approximately 20-year-old girl who had quite pale skin, black eyebrows and I think brown eyes and was wearing a light grey habit as if she were a nun, but she did not look like a modern-day nun but like pictures of women in religious orders from the tenth to the twelfth century. Her entire garment was very straight and covered her totally. The material looked quite thick.

Stewart

Julie and Stewart both thought it was a very powerful experience. Neither of them had ever tried this before and it was unlike anything either of them had ever experienced before. They have a very strong relationship and it's clear they have incarnated together in the past and chosen to do so again to learn from each other again. Their shared interest in a spiritual path is actually intensifying their experience and bringing them growth more quickly than is the case with most people.

Looking at your Current Life

I was once asked by the editor of a magazine why she should bother with past lives, as she had enough problems with this one. Can you imagine?! Surely it's clear: you sort out the past and those issues in the here and now are easier to deal with – aren't they?

Laurie Ann Lee explains how she feels her past life has affected her current one:

I am from Oklahoma in the USA and am currently engaged to a self-defined 'Welsh valley lad'. I work as a field communications dispatcher for a major utility company. I have no children, nor is giving birth a priority in my life. I am close to attaining two college degrees, one in psychology and the other in computer science. I have always (when focused) excelled in both school and professional work. Although I don't subscribe to any one organized religion, I do believe in a supreme power/nature/God.

Because I don't have any vivid memories of my past lives I can only go on instinct about how they've affected my current life. There's one aspect where I'm fairly certain that a past life has affected me, and that's my fear of heights. Other than tripping over the occasional pebble or street curb, I've never fallen from any sort of elevated level. Even when learning to ride a bike, I never once fell. I rode on my training wheels till I was 12 years old (embarrassing to say, but it does demonstrate my immense fear of falling, from an early age). I can't help but wonder if I died from a fall in a past life, as my earliest nightmares are all of falling.

Another way I think my past life has affected my current is that I rarely follow through with anything. Notice I said above 'I'm close to attaining two college degrees.' I've been two classes shy of those two degrees for over two years now and still haven't gone back to school. As a child, when racing I'd see the other kids get ahead of me and I'd just stop running. I can do pretty much anything – crotchet, embroider, play the piano, write, draw, speak – and if I pursued my talents I could be successful, but I get bored with things quickly and never have retained the motivation to take myself to higher levels. I can't count the chapters and first drafts of stories I've written, only for them to end up as scrap paper in the trash. I never get to the middle, let alone the end. This is a trait that I've always had and it confounds me. I have no idea why I cannot finish something – anything. I get almost to the end and then stop.

I've always been very outgoing, yet very insecure. I've always possessed a lot of guilt, from childhood onwards. So I go out of my way to express my feelings and be thoughtful, often to the detriment of my own needs.

I've also always feared that someone close to me will die without knowing what they mean to me. That's one thing that terrifies me about moving to the UK, though it's something I've always wanted to do. I fear leaving my grandmother, not being there for her should she need me. What would happen if she died when I wasn't there with her? What events would I miss sharing with her by moving? From a very young age, these worries have possessed my mind about anyone I love. Oddly, I've always found this to be a very morbid way of thinking, always worrying about unsaid words and unfulfilled deeds should a loved one die, but it's never been something that I have been able to quench.

Neither is worrying. I worry constantly and have done so from a very young age.

I remember being five years old and worrying about what would happen if someone died with things left unsaid. These aren't the normal thoughts of a five-year-old – not that I can truly define what is and isn't normal, but I never had any friends that felt the same way. Maybe as adults more of my peers would have an understanding of this through the losses they have experienced. No one died around me when I was five and there was nothing to trigger that level of worry and guilt over not having proper closure in relationships. And, oddly, in this life I rarely if ever have proper closure in any relationship. Though death hasn't been a predominant factor in my life, many of my relationships, especially in my early adult years, have ended very abruptly. One minute I'm kissing people goodbye as I would any other day and literally the next day they are out of my life for good. That's happened with my father and two fiancés. I can see how I could have developed the closure worries I have because of these relationships but, as I said, these were worries I experienced long before these events ever came to pass.

Fear is a huge factor in my life, yet the odd thing is that on the rare occasion I step out to conquer a fear, I most always have a very successful outcome. Nevertheless, fear rules me, fear and guilt. These feelings could have arisen as a result of this life, but they are characteristics I demonstrated prior to running into the situations that could have led to their development.

Laurie has some concerns that are common to us all, but there's an intensity and a wondering about past-life scenarios that have to be addressed. She says she never finishes anything, but in this case it may be *starting* something that's the issue. Perhaps she could have a past-life regression to answer some of these questions. Of course, nobody should feel pressured into anything, but it might just help to release some of her fears as well as open up her ability to follow things through.

If you, too, have questions or feel strongly that things you are encountering now are from a past life, it may be a good idea to trust your intuition, follow your heart and *have the regression!*

CHAPTER 4

RACHEL

OK, now you've seen other people's ways of doing past-life regression – maybe it's time to show you mine!

I use creative visualization. I relax my client and use a simple technique to help them into their past life and then I let them talk. First, though, I call on guides and angels to help and protect. I see the great archangels around me – Raphael in the east, Michael in the south, Gabriel in the west and Uriel in the north – standing in protection around the space I am working in. They are also sometimes seen in people's regressions, which never ceases to make me smile. You can use whatever method you wish, just do something to establish that link with the divine in you.

The first of the three case studies I'm going to share with you is that of Rachel. She and I met when she came to a hotel when I was filming *Most Haunted*. She had seen me on the show and had come to ask me if I would like to talk at Witchfest, a festival that's held every year and covers all manner of things from Wicca onwards. I was delighted to oblige and I am glad I did, as they turned out to be the most wonderful audience and I had one of the best days of my life there!

Rachel is Wiccan and very knowledgeable about spiritual matters. She is an extremely talented individual who makes the most of her Taurus gifts, with music and art at the fore. She has a husband and two lovely children and lives in the south of England. Her interest in past-life work fits in with her spiritual development, but she is wise enough to know that spiritual and earthly go hand in hand – an ethos I strongly subscribe to also. She knows that what you learn on your spiritual journey must be earthed or it's nothing more than dreams, but when I met her she seemed to have some reluctance about moving on as fast as I knew she could and indeed wanted to.

I took a look at her birth chart and it indicated past lives as a teacher in the spiritual arts. Her north node in Sagittarius suggested that she was here to pass that information on in this incarnation too and as it was in the third house, that was likely to be through writing, talking and singing – all of which she already did and I hope is going to do more of!

I visited her at her home, where all of her regressions took place.

Rachel

Session One

DW: Tell me when you feel, think or know you have landed.

R: OK, I'm there.

DW: What are you wearing on your feet?

R: Boots. They are shiny and sort of grey.

DW: Where are you?

R: England. It's the sixteenth century.

DW: Are you male or female?

R: Male.

DW: What age?

R: About 30, mid-thirties.

DW: What else are you wearing?

R: I have tights on, my name is Charles and I have long grey curly hair. I think it's a wig.

DW: Are you inside or outside?

R: Inside. The room has oak panels and there's a window. I'm looking out of it waiting, waiting for someone... It's a small house, but it has lots of rooms and some are quite grand.

There's a woman in a pale dress. The hips stick out from it. She's wearing a bonnet and she's about 30. She's panicking about something. I can hear a horse and cart coming. I'm in danger and she's trying to get me to leave. She's trying to protect me. She's not a lover, maybe a sister? She's very forceful.

I can hear horses' hooves. They are coming, people are coming, but I'm not afraid. I should run but I don't – I don't understand.

Another man is there now. He is dressed in red. I think he's a musketeer and he's coming for me. This is it. I won't survive this.

DW: What happens next?

R: I am climbing up onto the stocks, there are charges being read out against me – heresy dealing with astrology and the study of the occult. Someone has made this happen, turned me in.

I think my surname is Sampril, something like that. I have been helping someone involved in running the country. I can't see who or how they have made this happen to me.

I can see Elizabeth I. I don't know her, just see her. I can see a member of her court and a purse of money, money that's coming my way for some reason...?

I can also see one of Elizabeth's maids. I recognize her eyes – she's my daughter in this life. She is smiling.

DW: Why is she smiling?

R: I think she has something to do with getting me set free.

DW: What's happening now?

R: I can see a pomegranate! I think it's a symbol...? *[Pomegranates symbolize resurrection amongst many things and can be found in many cultures in religious paintings and embroidered onto holy robes.]* I am an old man now, there's sand by my feet. I lived by the sea *[she still does!]* and I am dying, starving, as I have no food. I have nowhere else to go, nothing else to do.

(Rachel reaches her death, for me a very important part of the regression. This is what happened next.)

DW: Move into the light, let it surround you. Now tell me what's happening.

R: I am back in the stocks. When they came to the house I was handed to a man wearing

47

red. I think he's a cardinal. He's mocking me. I can see Elizabeth I again. My relationship with the crown interfered with their purity. I don't think I knew Elizabeth – someone close to her, though.

In the light it's possible to talk to guides and perhaps astrals from this incarnation (astrals are the etheric part of humanity; they are our relations who have crossed, our friends in spiritual bodies free from the cumbersome physical bodies we lump around in!) and to sort out karmic responsibility and many more things besides, but Rachel chose to stop it there.

When asked what negative traits from that life she would like to leave behind, she chose to let go of the fear of balancing work with family.

The positive trait she chose to bring into her current life was dedication to her studies.

Elizabeth I had a very famous astrologer at court, John Dee, but no Charles Sampril or anything resembling it. However, records of that time are rare.

As for lessons learned, Rachel was shown she had ability and any reluctance was something that could be overcome. She was also shown where her reluctance could have come from, and once you know something like that, you can start to take steps towards resolving it, as Rachel in fact did.

Since her regression she has started a full-time job after taking a career break and is helping me teach some workshops – so that's positive, then!

Her link with her daughter was no surprise to her; she is well aware that family members often carry karmic conditions with them and it can be comforting to know they have been with us over the centuries – something that was to be of great significance to us as we went on.

Rachel

Session Two

DW: What are you wearing on your feet?

R: Black shoes, very highly polished. I am in London in the sixties – that's the 1960s. I'm wearing a grey suit, I can smell tobacco smoke and I live in a bedsit in west London.

DW: Where in west London?

R: I'm not sure. I am on my own in a room with a window, waiting – just like in the last regression. That's odd. I am waiting to go out. It's 11 a.m. and I have my briefcase and umbrella waiting.

DW: Do you know your name?

R: George, George B. Can't get the surname. I feel as if I am observing this man now. I feel as if I am floating.

DW: Give yourself time to settle. Just take your time and settle the energy.

R: I am walking down the road. There's something sinister about him. I know that in the briefcase there are documents – legal papers perhaps. Maybe he's a solicitor. I can hear cars going through puddles and see a road, but I am going to the Tube. I head down there. I have a bowler hat on, I'm very bitter and don't like the world – very grumpy.

I come out near Hyde Park. The sun is shining now and I am in a hurry to meet someone, excited about giving them some bad news!

DW: Go to your meeting and tell me what happens when you get there.

R: I am meeting a woman. She is short and pleasant looking. She looks like my mum does in old photos. I give her some documents. She is worried about them but I have no intention of giving her any comfort.

I'm not sure I *am* him, but there's something important about him.

He's getting older now.

I am now walking by the Thames. I've got lunch in my briefcase. I wouldn't go to a restaurant.

There's no family attached to this man. He doesn't know how to be generous.

There's something so familiar about him – is he a spirit guide?

DW: Just go with what you see, Rachel. We can debate it later.

R: OK. He's a very Mr Bean character, self-contained in an office at a desk. There are no photos on it.

Now I am in a hospital bed, wearing stripy pyjamas. It's an old hospital and I am very thin.

I still feel as if I am watching him rather than being him. It's very odd. He seems to have the energy of my son from my life now.

He's happy now, smiling at me, seems to feel free. What's left is a skeletal creature.

He had a bleak life as a child. His life was always that way. His job was to deliver bad news.

He has died now.

DW: Go into the light.

R: I know now that I wasn't him, I was his guide. I was watching him and although it felt as though I was him at the beginning, I was actually detached and I was watching him, supporting and loving him regardless of his grumpiness.

Now I can see a family member that I have a distant relationship with. She is behind me and I can't see her face-on.

I am now in a long arched tunnel. There are lots of doors leading off it. It's slightly scary and buzzing with power. It's a serious place.

I'm holding George's hand and he's a baby again. I stay with him a while. I feel like a ball of energy. I can hold the energy and control it. I am part of this place. I have a role to play. I must be cautious and respectful.

He's fading now, being absorbed. He's not afraid of moving on someplace else.

I can see a path, a path with trees. It's near where I grew up. I have reincarnated.

(At this point I ask Rachel to come back into the light.)

I can see a woman with flaming red hair, really mad hair. She is very stark. She shifts from earthly to ethereal. She's authoritative, guiding a lot of us. She helps me to decide to reincarnate, to explore a way to be whole.

DW: What negative thing do you want to leave behind?

R: Nothing.

(That's hardly surprising after a life truly living in the light, being a guide. I have experienced something similar and I too had nothing negative to leave behind from that life.)

DW: What positive things would you like to bring back, to remember?

R: I need to forgive myself for mistakes I have made. I see the number 444. I can see peacock feathers *[Rachel collects them in her current life]*. They form this woman's gown.

DW: Are you happy to leave that life now?

R: Yes.

Peacock feathers symbolize immortality, dignity, authority and compassion in different cultures – all qualities I would have thought this mysterious woman would have. But what do they mean for Rachel? What do you think? For me, they are about her ability to link into that authority, to recognize her own immortality, the immortality we all have through the survival of our soul. The woman with the peacock-feather gown was clearly a goddess-type figure, an embodiment of the eternal energy that is part of us all and that we are part of – something to think about.

It was interesting that Rachel had experienced a life as a spirit guide, a guide for the soul who is now her little boy in this life and who we now know had a not-that-great existence in his last incarnation. He is still a baby. How intriguing to see if he remembers anything, but one thing I can tell you: he isn't grumpy, he is a joyous smiley baby with mischief and wonder in his eyes – just as it should be!

People often assume their spirit guides couldn't have known them before, but remember you will drop your personality when the time is right and when you have adjusted to baring your soul you will want to take on the role of guide. Who better to guide than a soul you have loved on Earth and who better to have as a guide than someone who has loved you?

I have experienced this and I now know the person I guided in a previous life. Yet nowadays I hardly see her. We are still friends, but she is off doing her thing and I am doing mine. If she ever needed me I would be there like a shot, but I suspect that whatever bond of karma we shared it has now been negated and she is off creating more, as I am!

To go back to what Rachel experienced, the number 444 is an angelic number. See Doreen Virtue and Lynette Brown's book *Angel Numbers* (Hay House, 2005) for more. Doreen says:

Thousands of angels surround you at this moment, loving and supporting you. You have a very strong and clear connection with the angelic realm and are an Earth angel yourself.

You have nothing to fear, all is well.

Maybe that's it, maybe not! Rachel is still thinking that one through.

She had another regression which also proved very revealing:

Rachel

Session Three

DW: What are you wearing on your feet?

R: I am wearing lace-up shoes, black. I'm in an army uniform. It's khaki green. It's about 1941 and I have three stripes on my uniform. My name is Marion or Maureen Wilcox. I am in an air base. I think it's in Wiltshire. There are lots of people carrying gas masks and things. I think I am delivering a message. I'm not sure, but I do know I have a strong sense of purpose. I have my hair in a bun and I feel very much in control. I think I control the movement of the aircraft. I can see people planning flights. I am among them in a mansion somewhere. I have brought the plans to the airfield. A black car brought me here.

DW: What's happening now?

R: I can hear a siren going and feel people running around. I can hear propellers going and explosions.

I am worried about one of the pilots. I recognize him – he's my husband in my life now. I feel protective. How can I let them go up?

There are people on the phones, moving things around a board. I am in a single-storey building. It's all very temporary.

DW: Where are you now?

R: Back at a window. This time it's in my house and I am looking out into the garden. I am very alone; there aren't even any animals here. I am grieving. I expected life to be different, expected something else. I can see the roses in the garden. They have grown but my life hasn't.

The pilot who was shot down should have been my husband. His name was Donald, Donald...

I feel responsible. I created the plans that sent them out and I feel as if it's my fault. If only

I hadn't sent them, things would have been different and they wouldn't have crashed.

There's something about the garden, something pulling me towards it. I think I am going towards the pond. I want to die.

I cut my wrists and let them bleed into the water. It feels unreal – maybe it's symbolic?

I think I'm dying, falling asleep. It's going all white.

DW: What's happening now?

R: I can see a child with her hand out, standing still. She's not going to go through the door. I feel as if she is on a platform at a station with steam trains like they have in Harry Potter. She doesn't know where to go. Is this me? She's waiting to be told what to do, where to go.

The girl has gone, she wasn't me, she just brought me here. Now a man is waving, showing me where to go and what to do.

Another train is taking me back to the house, full circle. It's bizarre, I feel as if I am a ghost, floating around the house afraid to go on – maybe because I took my own life? Regret perhaps?

I haunt this house. Other people blame me. It was in my power to change things, but it's

Groundhog Day now, a cycle over and over again.

(I ask Rachel to move on a bit.)

There are sunflowers in the garden. I hadn't noticed them before. It's something different – the cycle has been broken and I don't have to do the same thing any more.

I am back in the tunnel, like in the last regression. I don't feel afraid any more, I feel like an adult, and I can see a small boy. I am protecting him. *[This life would have been just before Rachel was a guide in the last regression.]* I can feel him around and then he disappears.

DW: What's happening now?

R: I want to be reborn but not yet. I am still waiting for the little boy to pull away. I feel sad. He wants to play. We do play just one last time.

I feel as if I am me now. I can feel all the creative things I can be. I can feel it!

There's an old man to my right. He may be my paternal grandfather. I never knew him. He wants to say hello even though he has never met me before.

DW: What negative thoughts do you want to let go of, Rachel?

R: Blame – I need to let go of the feeling that I am to blame.

DW: What positive things can you learn and bring forward?

R: Lots of self-belief – I need to bring that back and I think I am beginning to feel that. I can feel it in my solar plexus.

Rachel hates airports and the thought of flying in this life, and the sound of a siren scares her. Now she knows why and can start to work on letting go of those fears.

Suicide is always a tough subject in past-life work. There is nothing you can do or say to your client when they see it coming. Rachel followed the same pattern as most people in that situation – as soon as she released herself from her own repetitive cycle and let herself go into the light, things changed. Interestingly, she spent several years volunteering as a Samaritan in her early twenties, being filled with the desire to help people in crisis. Perhaps engaging in that work was motivated by her experience in her past life.

There were several themes in Rachel's lives, the most obvious being letting go of blame, forgiving herself and accepting she couldn't be in control of everything. Her family was also very evident. It seems she and her immediate family have close karmic links, which is pretty normal, but Rachel's seem closer than most – comforting to know in this case. They are a strong and happy unit, which is born from familiarity and lessons learned in past lives, I suspect.

Rachel is now balancing her home life with a new full-time career, has lost some weight and is looking great! She has been running her past-life work alongside other personal development therapy, with the therapist's full support and knowledge, and is well on her way to gaining the control and happiness she so richly deserves in this life.

Here are her own comments on her regressions:

Although I have been studying and practising Wicca since 1992, I had never had a past-life regression before. The entire process, which was led by David at my home, was a magickal and extraordinary experience that I will never forget.

As David guided me through a series of visualizations which began the regression, I was surprised at the feeling of energy that filled me and the sensation of floating as if my body and mind had been waiting for me to unlock this knowledge for many years. When I began to speak, my voice felt distant and the words flowed without any conscious thought. I saw images of people and places in my mind and had a light tingling sensation in my third-eye area. What I found most astounding, however, were the strong emotions that I felt during the regressions. I shed tears of both sadness and joy from my closed eyes, and when I felt fear at one point, my legs physically shook.

David managed the session very well, helping me to ground myself when the intensity became too much and guiding me through some of the more difficult memories.

Although after the regressions I found it hard to remember the exact details of what I had said due to the words coming from beyond my conscious mind, I felt that I had gained a new understanding of myself on a subconscious level and of some of the fears and motivations that are with me in this incarnation. The work has helped me at least rationalize some of my fears, such as of flying, and has provided me with a lot of inspiration for further mystical and creative work. I have always wanted to teach and

*this work also gave me the courage I need-
ed to move on to the next level and conduct
workshops with David.*

Rachel is a very powerful lady and part of recogniz-
ing that power in herself has come from the journey
her past lives have taken her on. Now it's up to her
to put what she has learned into action and I am
sure she will. Unlocking that part of her memory
will bring a new insistence, a new drive to use what
she has always had.

CHAPTER 5

YOUR TURN...

Fascinating as others' stories are, they aren't your story, your proof. Now it's your turn to find out what it's like!

The first thing to say is that it's actually different for everyone. We all see things differently and how you feel in a regression depends on your own personality, soul and spirit.

It's important not to set yourself unrealistic standards when you go into past-life regression and compare yourself unfavourably to others. This is something I feel strongly about: you shouldn't compare yourself to anyone – you are unique and should be proud of it, and in case you're not getting the message here, I am of course not talking solely about past-life regression!

Here's something to remind you of that – another visualization. You know you want it.

Get comfy.

Breathe in on the count of four, hold it for two, breathe out for four and hold it for two – do that three times.

Now imagine you're in a forest – any forest you like. Just really see yourself there. It's night-time. Imagine the trees, the smells that surround you, the temperature, the animals that may be close by. You can see the full moon above you. It's a clear night and the stars are shining brightly – very, very brightly.

There's a path ahead of you in the forest. Follow that path until you come to a clearing. In the distance you can see an oak tree shimmering in the moonlight, a living, breathing tree.

Go into the clearing and stand with the tree behind you.

Now lie down on the grass.

Feel the earth underneath you, the slight dampness of night on your skin and the cool, crisp air around you.

Now look at the stars.

Look at the bright ones, the not-so-bright and the shooting stars... Look at the twinkling of those stars...

As you gaze up into the sky you see a bright star in the east, brighter than all the rest. It's moving across the sky.

As you watch it, it stops directly over you, shining brightly and bathing you in its light.

Let that silver sparkling energy wash all over you. Giggle if you like – it's tickly! Let it fall into every part of your being, reminding you that you have your own star, a star to guide you and to help you shine.

Now look at the star again. It's moving away towards the west, but you know it's always there for you.

As it goes, make a wish. Wish upon your own star and remind yourself your dreams will come true because you now know you can follow your own star rather than compare yourself to any other.

Spend some time just dreaming.

Now prepare to leave this place.

Get up, feeling lighter and brighter, happy to walk back along your path into the midst of the forest.

As you walk along the path, let it melt away and bring your consciousness back into the here and now...

Kettle on, biscuits out. Write down how you feel and what you're going to do to make your dreams come true.

After your visualization you might feel a little heavy or perhaps a little elated. Either way, it's important to acknowledge how you feel. It's also important to ground yourself, to bring yourself back into the physical world, which is why I recommend a cup of tea and a biscuit. There are other things you can do, too. Have a bath and put some salt in the water, do some gardening, have a glass of wine or get a little closer to the one you love – all are valid! The more you practise, the more you'll know how to cope with your energy. It's always about practice and technique.

And now you know how special you are, let's find out who you've been...

The Akashic Records

Some of you will already have heard of these. They are a cosmic library where you can review your own personal journey in an intellectual rather than emotional way. I tend to take people to the Akashic records in group regressions as it brings the mind into play rather than the emotions, making the situation much easier to control.

For those of you who haven't done much in the way of meditating or creative visualization, there's a lot more on this in my books *Complete Guide to*

Developing Your Psychic Skills and *Past, Present and Future* (Hay House, 2006 and 2007), and if you can't remember the way, there's a CD of meditations to help you too. It's called *Meditations to Explore Your Past Lives* (Hay House, 2008).

For now, don't worry – you can do it! In the following visualization, I'll take you to the Akashic records and you can get a glimpse of a past life. Are you ready?

Take some time out in a favourite spot and begin.

Close your eyes and breathe in deeply. Hold the breath and let it out, and as you do so, relax your shoulders and let that feeling flow down through your entire body. Feel relaxed.

*Imagine you're in your forest. See it around you. Build it as if you're really there. In fact, you **are** there!*

Walk along the path that unfolds ahead of you. Follow it until you come to a large oak tree, a tree that has a door in its base. Go through the door when it opens for you, taking you into a room whose floor is covered in black and white tiles and strewn with herbs, herbs like rosemary and lavender that release their scent as you walk on them.

Now move towards the back of the room where you will see an altar covered in a simple white cloth.

Burning in the centre of it is a single blue flame. Pause here and ponder the journey you're about to take.

Then look up and see in front of you three doors. Walk towards the one on the left.

As you approach, it opens and on the other side you see an orange globe, a sphere of swirling light. Step inside it. As you do so, it begins to rise up. Don't worry, you're perfectly safe. Just enjoy the peace and calm that surround you as you move through the ether.

Gently you feel the sphere land and almost as soon as you do it melts away to reveal a frozen landscape, a desert of ice and snow in which there appears to be another path ahead of you. This time it's strewn with words, phrases, poetry and musical notes. Follow the path.

Ahead of you there's an almighty rumble and in the near distance you see a giant library rise up from the ice. It's circular and surrounded by stairs leading up to pillars which have doors behind them – lots of stairs, pillars and doors.

Move towards the doorway you are drawn to. Walk carefully, but be sure of your intention.

Move up to the door and take note of what it's like. Are there any engravings on it?

The door will open and you will find yourself in a hallway. Either side of this hallway there are artefacts from your past lives. Have a look and try to remember some of them, as they offer some clues to where you have lived before.

Move towards yet another door at the back of the hallway and wait until your Akashic guide comes to greet you.

Your guide will take you through the door and into a large library. Follow them to a desk on which lies a book. Thank them for their attendance and turn your attention to the book. What does it look like? Is there a name on it? Touch it. How does it feel?

The book will open and reveal whatever it has to reveal to you. Spend five minutes of silence with it. That may not seem like long, but it will be ample, and once you learn the route you can come back whenever you feel the need.

When you are ready to leave, allow your book to close and follow your Akashic guide out of the library.

At the door thank them for their help and once more walk down your hallway, taking note of anything you might have missed on the way in.

Leave the Akashic records and go down the steps and back into your orange sphere. Let it surround

*you and take you back to the room at the bottom
of your tree.*

*Walk out of the room and back into your forest.
Follow the path and as you move along it, let it
melt away and slowly bring your consciousness back
to the here and now!*

Kettle on, biscuits out and pen in hand!

Here are two past lives that were found using this technique. Janette comes from Essex. She's single, has three ponies and one dog. She is a healer and also sits in a psychic development circle. She works for an animal feed Internet company. These are the past lives she experienced:

I was a 19-year-old girl, 5 ft tall, fair, slim and blue-eyed. My name was Emily Patterson and my nickname was Emi. I lived with my parents and younger sister in a small town in Ireland. It was September 1650. We lived in a small cottage in the village. I wore a light brown skirt and a fitted bodice with a square neck, a cotton blouse and a small cap. I had my hair up.

I have never been to Ireland and did not know of the town until I found it on the map. The clothes I found myself wearing do fit the period. I saw my sister as a child in that life, but I never told her about it. Then she took a trip to the Akashic records herself and told me of a village and valley which I knew and of a cart and horses out of control.

In the second past-life regression I was male, about 28 years old, 5 ft 10 inches tall, a Native American with shoulder-length hair in a small plait each side to hold it out of the way. I was married and my wife was about 26 years old and small. I had three children – a girl twelve years old, another about nine years old and a boy five years old. I wore a light blue tunic and pale leather trousers. We had one horse and seemed to live fairly well.

Past-life regression has changed my whole outlook on death. When I viewed my death in the first life it gave me an understanding of how the soul leaves the body and lives on. The second death made me realize why I always put other people first and often go without myself (my sister gets angry with me over this) – it's because my family suffered after my death in that life. I can't make up for that now, but I can try to heal it and treat myself without feeling guilty. That death also showed me the strong connection between me and my guide Ben.

I never really knew if I believed in past lives before, but with the regressions it was as though someone had turned on a light. Past-life regression has changed my life and has helped with my healing and development in the circle. My whole outlook on life has changed and I am a much calmer person now.

Janette got a lot of information from visiting the Akashic records rather than a full regression, which shows the power of this magical journey when done with sound intent. She took her lives to the death; something I advise not just because you see how the story ends but, as Janette rightly says, it changes your outlook and brings peace. That was very much in evidence when I had my first regression.

It's also interesting that Janette has formed a stronger bond with her guide now as well as realizing she deserves a treat or two.

Janette went on to find out about more past lives. Here's another one from her, showing the benefits of following the story of your soul...

I found myself in Turkey. I was ten years old and had been born in 1250. I was the youngest of three boys. Our father was a merchant.

I had a happy childhood, but then things began to change.

My oldest brother became a soldier when he was 14 years old. The day he left I cried, somehow knowing I would never see him again. Three years later we received a message to say he was dead. My mother just cried and cried.

About a year later, when I was myself about 14 years old, it was decided that I too would join the army, and my brother, who was a year older, would work for our father. Leaving home was hard, but I did as I was told.

Time passed and I became a good soldier. At the age of 20 I married and two sons followed quickly, but the holy lands were under threat from the Franks – that was the name given to Christians – and two years later we marched to Damascus. The crusades were in full swing and we had to defend our god, our country and our holy lands.

I saw my first battle within days, which was the day I killed for the first time. I cut the man's throat and it was so easy. The battle raged and one soon became ten.

After that day the battles began to merge. Soon ten lives became twenty and then I lost count. I was a good soldier fighting for my god. I was cold and brutal, finishing off prisoners and survivors without a thought. I saw many souls I know now in my present life. We weren't all on the same side, but we were all killing for our religion.

I managed to survive for many years because I was so brutal and cold. I don't know how I died, but I am sure it was violent. Perhaps I am not ready to face it.

I never knew Turkey took part in the crusades until I did some research; the ninth crusade started about 1270. After the meditation I made notes on my uniform and sword. I had a type of skirt made of leather straps which hung down, a breastplate of small leather squares and a helmet a bit like a turban with a pointed top, which are all historically correct. My sword was wide and curved like a crescent moon, which I have been told is called a Cairo.

I have always thought that religious war is wrong. In my eyes, whatever god or goddess you worship, murder in the name of religion is wrong. Although I would always defend my family, I have never felt the need to defend my beliefs. Now they are pagan, with a little bit of Qabalah and Spiritualism mixed in, and I feel that even if people don't understand them, that's their problem, not mine. Everyone has the right to believe in what they want.

Many of the souls I saw in that Turkish life now belong to my healing circle. We are a mix of all belief systems but never question each other's beliefs. I think that I had actually learned my lesson from that life before I even knew of it. When I sit in the circle I sometimes lead a PLR meditation and see what the participants see and often get the point of those lives (I never lead, just listen) – can I develop this?

Here we see that Janette has researched some great facts and got her own personal proofs. It is very important to cultivate your personal belief in future regressions in this way.

This past life is interesting considering what a gentle, peaceful and healing individual Janette is now – is that because she is balancing the violence from her previous life or has her soul been sickened by that experience and now knows better?

Janette can most definitely develop her ability to see other people's lives, and what a joy to see her listening and not leading – it is so very important not to put anything into people's subconscious minds as you work.

I have met some people from Janette's healing circle and they are indeed lovely, lovely souls drawn together for the greater good – a display of karma in action, that force that brings people together for so many reasons.

Which brings us to...

CHAPTER 6

SOUL LINKS

In life, there are some people we choose to be around and some we seem to be lumbered with! Of course, the truth is we choose to be around them all, even those who challenge us to distraction, and these are usually the ones we learn most from.

These choices may continue down the ages like a chain reaction. If everything we do or say can create karma, it stands to reason that this karma is probably best negated with those we know, those who would be more likely to agree to help us, than with random individuals who might or might not keep up their end of the bargain when we incarnate.

Does it mean we always incarnate with the same souls? Maybe not, maybe we have a rest in between teaching each other a lesson, but that doesn't mean that even when we haven't incarnated with someone we can't make our presence felt. We can make it felt from behind the veil...

Here's an example that was sent to me. The writer prefers to remain anonymous.

On 22 July 2006, my friends and I were sitting in a meditation circle, although we had decided not to sit for too long. Towards the close of the circle I suddenly heard the name 'Thomas Moore' being shouted over and over to me. I asked if anyone knew anybody of this name, but nobody could place it.

The following morning, I awoke to poetry repeatedly being 'sung' through my head. I was unable to shake this off, so I sat down at my dressing table to write down the words. As I did so, I looked around and saw a young man in Regency dress smiling and I felt overcome by a deep love. Then my hand suddenly felt as if it were being guided – I felt as if I was becoming this man. The writing flowed for some time.

As I was sitting there my daughter came to tell me she was going out and I replied, 'Fly free, little bird, fly free, but make sure you come home to me!' This turned out to be very significant, as I have since found from one of Thomas Moore's journals that his wife, Bessy, used this phrase to him when he was going away from home.

When I went downstairs, my dog barked at me repeatedly and I felt astounded by the television and all the modern technology, and confused. I had a strong sense of disorientation.

Thomas remained very close to me, sending poetry of love, nature, politics and spirituality sometimes up to five times a day. Many times thereafter I was overcome by tears, as I still am to this day when he draws very close, and would quite often use old English speech in everyday conversation! For me this was a learning curve, as many of the words used by Thomas in his poems would not have been used naturally by me. Often I would look these words up in the dictionary to clarify their meaning in the context of the poem.

During this time I met a lady through a Spiritualist church. We got on very well and I always looked forward to seeing her. One day she told me that she had had a regression. I hasten to add she knew nothing of my experience with Thomas, as I kept this very private. What she started to tell me absolutely astounded me! In her past life she was a man by the name of John Russell, who unbeknown to her was a close friend of Thomas and Bessy!

Halfway through her story I stopped her and told her I knew of whom she was talking and explained why. She was just as amazed as I was! She is also an astrologer and has done my chart and those of Tom and Bessy and explained that they are closely linked.

As the poems became more intimate and the emotional link with Thomas stronger, I was introduced to a lady who did past-life regression. I took the opportunity and was regressed. I found myself in Regency clothes as a young woman as Thomas held his hand outstretched towards me, shrouded within the mists of time. I was Bessy, his wife... I cried silent tears throughout the session and apparently spoke with a different voice. I felt that I had arrived home.

Memories have remained with me from the regression, such as a ring Thomas gave to me during that time. I later noticed the same one whilst browsing through an antiques window and promptly bought it.

Thomas later sent me a poem about stars during a stay in Wiltshire, then later that night he told me to look out of the window and within a minute I watched a shooting star go by.

The poems that I received from Thomas gave evidence regarding his family, his beliefs, personal experiences and then the spiritual side of his life now in spirit. I refused to read any of his original printed poems until I knew I would not receive any more from him in spirit. There are many similarities between the two sets of poems which have since become apparent.

My husband changed his job and subsequently found his new job would take him to see clients based in the area around where Bessy and Thomas lived for 30 years. Each time I go with him I am overcome emotionally, but I always have a feeling of peace, as if I have arrived home. I visit their grave, which is a peculiar feeling. The first time I went to the church, I did not need to look for the grave. I found it instantly. I just knew where it was.

It was the same with their former home – I recognized the chimneys and the position of the house from afar. I felt as though it was my home and wanted so much to go inside. Since the regression I feel that I cannot go back again, as it would fill me with deep sadness with the memories I now have.

I have read four volumes of Thomas's memoirs since the regression. As I read, 'memories' would come back. I began to see visions of our children, for example a little girl at a table drinking milk. I later found that Thomas wrote that after their daughter died, Bessy would dream of her sitting like this. Before I had my second daughter I would have continuous dreams where I held a baby girl in my arms. It seemed so real I would wake up crying and feel depressed when I realized it was just a dream. Bessy and Tom lost a baby girl at seven to eight months old and Thomas recorded that Bessy had disturbing dreams of holding her baby after their loss.

Bessy seems to have suffered from the same medical conditions as I have, even down to having an abscess/boil on her leg for some time at the same age, painful sinuses and even the same dental problems! Her personality appears very much like mine from the little I have read about her and I would even go as far to say we look very similar too. Apparently, Thomas and Bessy gave their first daughter the nickname of 'Boo Boo' which, I hate to say it now, I gave to an ex of mine...

Whilst I was standing in a meadow one day, Tom told me to look down and said, 'Look for the four-leaved clover.' The field was full of clover, but I looked down and there it was, at the end of my shoe! The next week when I was sitting in the garden on the lawn he told me to lift my hand, which I did. Underneath were three four-leaved clovers! 'One for each of you now,' he said. (We are a family of four!)

Thomas was Irish and when I was younger, during the Troubles, I was very sympathetic to the Irish cause (although not the violence and bloodshed, I hasten to add). I felt very strongly about it, although I have no Irish links as far as I know in my family. Dublin was a place I longed to go to.

Another time, as I was going to sleep, Thomas said he was going to send me a birthday present. My birthday is in July and this was November. I reminded him of this, but he replied, 'No, this birthday, this month.' I remembered then that Bessy was born in November. The next day I went to visit a friend. Whilst there I was instantly drawn to a beautiful print picture. She said she had two the same and I could have the other, as she didn't know where to put it. As she went upstairs I read the inscription on the bottom and it was entitled 'Cupid and Psyche'. This is very significant as Bessy was nicknamed Psyche (because of her beauty) by Samuel Rogers, a close friend of theirs at the time.

Tom also said once he would send me a gold locket and then my husband bought me a surprise anniversary gold locket. He had set out to buy a silver one, but no silver ones had been in stock. He knew nothing of Tom's promise.

I always wanted three daughters when I was younger and worried about having boys. This I now feel was due to the fact that Tom and Bessy lost three young daughters and one of their older sons caused them problems.

Tom and Bessy lived at a place once called 'The Cedars' and I have lived on a road called 'The Cedars'!

Tom had a close friend with the surname of Godfrey. I also have a close friend with that surname.

Bessy had two sisters, as I do, and she was a dancing actress on the stage, which is what I aspired to be through ballet when I was a teenager. I always regretted not following it through. Bessy had to give it up when marrying.

The list is endless.

I have always enjoyed looking around National Trust properties and stately homes. I always felt drawn to them and now I feel I know why.

I have always wanted to live in the south rather than the north of England and Tom and Bessy lived in the south.

When I was about ten years old I would sit day after day drawing pictures of ladies in nineteenth-century dress. I was always drawn to the nineteenth century and, again, now I know why.

To this day my life has been enriched spiritually by the connection. I now love classical music, for example. Occasionally I go to the Spiritualist church and have had lovely messages from Tom. Once he mentioned my past-life name and talked briefly of the life he had had.

I feel very blessed that reincarnation has been proved to me in so many fantastic and so many unexpected ways!

Thomas walks alongside me in this life, as I know he did before.

I leave you with a poem he sent to me:

THE STARLIT SKY

Pull back that curtain
And pass through time
And look unto that starlit sky!
That starlit sky that shines so bright
That brings its sparkle
Unto the night.

Come, take my hand,
Pass through the veil
And look to where the moon doth sail.
Do not be afraid
To look to the past
Just step aside
The shadows cast.

And bridge that gap
Of times gone by
When thee cast thy eyes
To that starlit sky!

Please dance with me
Along the way.
Remember times
Of yesterday.
For nought is lost
But dreams to cherish,
For this love of ours
It could not perish!

What an extraordinary experience.

The reason this person wants to remain anonymous is clear – they are concerned about people assuming it's all made up and perhaps subjecting them to ridicule, and that's perfectly understandable. It's not easy when you have a link to a famous life, as there are those who will always trot out the 'Aren't they always famous?' line. As you can see from this book, no, they are not, that is an urban myth put about by those who know little about the subject.

The links between lives here are interesting, but do they prove a past-life connection? Could they simply be coincidence? One thing or maybe three or four things might be written off as chance, but there's a very long list here. Proof was also sent via an outside source to this person, someone who would have shared some aspects of this past life. That's another piece in the jigsaw and reinforces the idea that we travel with the same people from one life to another.

Can past lives really reach out into your current incarnation to the point where they can even affect birthday gifts? It's extraordinary, but I have learned that nothing is beyond the realms of possibility and when the time is right such proofs can and do appear.

Now read the poem again and think about past lives – does it say something else to you now? Is

Thomas writing about a starlit sky or a past-life attachment?

Compare the poem to this one by Thomas Moore:

COME, REST IN THIS BOSOM

Come, rest in this bosom, my own stricken deer,
Though the herd have fled from thee, thy home is still here:
Here still is the smile that no cloud can o'ercast,
And the heart and the hand all thy own to the last.

Oh! what was love made for, if 'tis not the same
Through joy and through torments, through glory and shame!
I knew not, I ask not if guilt's in that heart,
I but know that I love thee, whatever thou art!

Thou hast call'd me thy angel, in moments of bliss, –
Sill thy Angel I'll be, 'mid the horrors of this, –
Through the furnace, unshrinking, thy steps to pursue,
And shield thee, and save thee, or perish there too!

Is the style similar? I will leave you to ponder on that and to think about whether a life remembered with a link to fame is harder or easier to accept for the person being regressed and those around them. If it were you, would you tell anyone?

What about the other way round – what if you once shared a life with someone who is famous now? How would you go about telling them?!

Jenny Smedley explains:

The nightmares I suffered were graphic, extraordinarily real and very frightening. They always ended up with me screaming out to someone called Ryan for help. Even after I'd woken up I would be trembling with fear and edgy for the rest of the day.

The first nightmare depicted a rape and seemed very real. I knew it was more than a random nightmare and I lived in fear for years that it would turn out to be a premonition and something that would really happen to me one day. I could still see the man's face when I woke up, in every detail – his dirty teeth, long greasy hair and pock-marked skin – and it would make me shudder. This man was real and not something from my imagination. Even though I knew that Ryan, whoever he was, was coming, I wondered if when it happened, he'd be in time to save me.

When this all came to a head in 1995, the nightmares were only part of the depression I was experiencing. Even my wonderful husband Tony was at a complete loss as to how to help me. Despite having my dream house, horses and land and the best son and husband, there was a shadow hanging over me.

As my inexplicable depression deepened, the feeling of loss grew, the nightmares became more frequent and the questions became more intense. Who was Ryan? Why was I calling to him for help?

One day, as I was wandering aimlessly through a shopping mall, shrouded in a haze of sadness, feeling totally cut off from those around me, I passed a butcher's shop. As the meat cleaver fell into a side of beef, suddenly I fell into a waking vision. A broadsword wielded by a kilted warrior plunged into a dark-haired man and I knew the mortally wounded man was Ryan. I flashed back to reality and had a lot of trouble even making it back to my car, staggering on wobbly legs. So the nightmares had started intruding into my waking hours. It was terrifying. Was I going insane?

The depression became dangerous as I sat at home alone, the spectre of suicide calling to me, offering an escape. I didn't know which way to turn. I've come to realize since that often, in order to accept and grasp what we must, we have to be squeezed this way. Somehow the pressure opens our hearts and souls to what we need to know.

And so it was with me. One day while Tony was at work I was watching TV in our English home when a man's face appeared on the screen. It sort of stuck there as the picture rolled round and round. I stared at a pair of blue eyes, transfixed. Just like that, in a second, this stranger – for I had never seen him before – swept away my depression and changed my entire life. When people had said to me previously that something had changed their lives in a second, I'd found it hard to believe, but that's what happened to me. In that second my depression fled, never to return, even though I had no idea why. My every waking hour was filled with joy instead of misery and every little chore just made me glad to be alive. My husband and son were astonished and overjoyed at the changes in me. But it was to be many more months before I discovered why I felt that way and the whole truth of the story.

Another 'stranger' suggested to me that the man was someone I'd known in a past life, and when I heard that, something clicked in my mind. This was right, this was true, I just knew it. Hypnotic regression was suggested and it revealed a passionate and tragic story.

As I sunk into a hypnotic trance I was transported back to my past life in the seventeenth century and finally discovered who Ryan was...

Ryan Fitzgerald was born James Ryan in southern Ireland in the early 1600s. He had a twin sister, Elspeth, and older sister, Patricia, and their mother, Caitlin, was married to a man called John Ryan, but the twins had actually been sired by the Earl of Kildare, Thomas Fitzgerald. When John Ryan discovered this, he left his wife and children, including his own daughter, Patricia, despite the fact that Fitzgerald had died before the twins had even been born.

Caitlin died from overwork when James was just 12 years old. Although he did his best to support his two sisters, inevitably, when neither help nor acknowledgement from his half-brother, the Fitzgerald heir, was forthcoming, the two girls succumbed to malnutrition and disease.

After that, James Ryan became a rebel. He took the two surnames of his families and called himself Ryan Fitzgerald to inform the whole world that he was Fitzgerald's bastard son. An old gatekeeper gave him his father's seal ring, which would prove his heritage. This earned Ryan a death warrant. He fled to England, running for his life from the Fitzgerald clan.

Several years later, after finding work where he could on farms and smallholdings, he ended up in Hambledon. Walking along the lane leading to the estate of the de Porte family, he came across Madeleine de Porte as two ruffians were assaulting her.

I remembered being Madeleine, the aristocratic daughter of Edwin and Rebecca de Porte. Rebecca had died when I was six years old and my father remarried four years later. His new wife Margaret and I had never got along, as I had always believed that she had married him solely for his money and position. But eventually an uneasy truce had developed between us. This peace was shattered forever when Ryan Fitzgerald appeared on the scene.

Ten years after my father's remarriage, I was out riding my horse alone. Hampered by my long dress and riding too fast, I was struck on the head by a branch and knocked unconscious to the ground. While I lay helpless, two youths took advantage of my befuddled state and tried to molest me. Coming across the drama by chance, Ryan drove them away, saving me from disgrace. When I came round and found Ryan watching me, I was terrified of him for a moment, but as soon as our eyes met I felt no more fear, only love, instantaneous and eternal.

I took my hero home and was dismayed when my parents treated him like a criminal. My defence of him was total and unshakeable. Margaret and Edwin could see the danger signs and tried to keep us apart, but it was too late. I had found my love and would never let him go.

Despite his efforts to resist me, as he knew that it would bring my parents' anger down on him, Ryan's love for me constantly tormented him until he finally admitted it to me. When he asked me to marry him, I accepted readily, for it was my dearest wish and I thought that marriage to me would keep him safe.

Even though Margaret had him beaten to within an inch of his life, Ryan's love, once declared, couldn't be unwritten, and despite Margaret's threats, we got married in secret and then returned together to face my parents' wrath. From that day, Ryan no longer kept the seal ring secret and wore it as a wedding band.

On my ongoing voyage of discovery, I recalled many episodes during the three years that Ryan and I spent together. The reality of one of the nightmares I'd suffered was revealed – it took place when Ryan just saved me from a rapist. All this time Margaret and Edwin resorted to all manner of trickery and treachery to destroy the love Ryan and I felt for each other and I saw many of the attempts made by Margaret to be rid of the Irishman. She loathed him because he had thwarted her plans to marry me to a rich old man whose fortune could soon swell the family coffers.

It became clear that Ryan and I could not be parted save by death, so eventually Margaret brought death to him. Ryan and I were forcibly torn from each other's arms and Edwin used his political clout to have Ryan conscripted into the English army and sent into battle against the Scottish, where he was killed.

I'd witnessed his death many times in my nightmares and visions, but there was a mystery surrounding it that took some time to solve. In my vision, the kilted warrior, whom I assumed to be Scottish, after striking the fatal blow, reached down and tore the ring from Ryan's limp hand. As he took it, he said, 'This was my father's!' I didn't understand this for some years. Finally I met a man who had shared the same dream and he was the reincarnation of Ryan's half-brother. He had been racked with guilt for years in his current life, without understanding why. It turned out that the soldier who had killed Ryan was wearing an Irish, not Scottish, kilt and he had come across the Irish Sea to track Ryan down and reclaim the seal ring. He had gone to the house in Hambledon and been put onto Ryan's trail by Margaret. She had no doubt been gleeful at adding certainty rather than chance to her intent to see Ryan dead.

In another nightmare I saw my descent into despair after Ryan's sudden loss. Locked in a room for two days and nights after his disappearance, going insane with terror at what might be happening to him, my fate was sealed. Once I was released, I roamed the woodland where Ryan and I used to walk, and lay down in the long grass where we used to lie together. I saw his spirit many times, walking in his beloved bluebells, laughing, loving. I could not live without him and, believing I could see his ghost, I followed it up to the attic of the house. Looking down to the courtyard below and seeing an image of Ryan with his arms outstretched, I jumped to him and to my death. My last word was 'Ryan!'

Tony and I searched for evidence of this past life and we found it. We visited the church in Milton Abbas where Ryan and Madeleine had been married and the house in Hambledon where they had lived. It was no surprise to discover that the house was haunted by the footsteps of a man coming down the wooden back stairs which in the present day are no longer there! When the occupiers opened the door, to their astonishment one of the first things I asked was, 'Have you found the secret room yet?' I was able to say where it was, and it had taken them years to find it.

The man on the TV, who was almost identical to Ryan, turned out to be someone called Garth Brooks. I'd never seen him or heard of him because I wasn't a country music fan and country music was pretty much unpublicized and even derided in England at that time. This one-off concert that I'd just 'happened' to catch was very much the exception on English TV. Of course, after that I looked into the music of Garth Brooks and later became astonished at the number of his lyrics that resonated with his past life as Ryan Fitzgerald.

With Tony's support and Madeleine's spirit pushing me on, I was finally able to close the circle by reconnecting the two of us. This meant I had to fly to the USA and find Garth Brooks. I also had to get to meet him and find the courage to tell him my story. What would he think? How would he react? I think the photo of us meeting says it all. They say a picture paints a thousand words and this one has moved people to tears. What Garth said that day will remain a secret, unless he chooses to reveal it.

Extraordinary 'coincidences' popped up after our meeting and after I had written the story in a book. Garth 'invented' a character called Chris Gaines, and made a 'pop' album under that name. The media ridiculed this ploy, as they didn't understand the premise at all. It turned out that in numerology, the names Chris Gaines and Ryan Fitzgerald added up to the same base number. The birth date 'invented' for Gaines and the real birth date for Ryan Fitzgerald also added up to the same base number. Garth's 'disguise', including clothes and wig when being Gaines, closely resembled those of Ryan. Perhaps this was how Ryan re-emerged in Garth's mind.

Garth saved a child from grass fire in Oklahoma. The boy was called Ryan. The fire was a direct reflection of the forest fire fought by Ryan in the 1600s.

Ryan was killed by a broadsword that penetrated his abdomen. Garth even 'recreated' this in a car crash when a piece broke off from the car's body and ran him through, almost killing him. He bears the scar today.

Garth co-wrote and recorded a song called Ireland. The lyrics tell of a young Irishman fighting and dying in someone else's war in another land.

This whole experience changed my life in incredible ways. I became an award-winning songwriter, even though I had never written a song before. I also became an author, magazine columnist, TV presenter and feature *writer. From being a sad, overweight, depressed housewife who hadn't worked for 25 years, I became a confident, spiritually aware, slimmer woman who counselled people on their spiritual needs. I am now blessed to be able to repay Tony for all his years of sacrifice and support by earning enough as a writer to support us both.*

If you'd like to read the whole story, Souls Don't Lie *(O Books, 2006) is available from Amazon and all good bookstores.*

Jenny is an extraordinary woman and, as she says, she's a very busy writer, columnist and television presenter. All of those roles take a certain confidence, which Jenny clearly has.

Her story is fascinating and I know how absolutely genuine she is, but how would you feel if she'd told her story without the link to Garth Brooks? Would you have been as interested? I would have been, simply because her proofs aren't about Garth being a famous man in this incarnation, they are about how she felt, how the experience affected this life, who else was around her and the way in which the information came into her life.

Thank you, Jenny, for being so open and for the wonderful work you do on this subject.

We'll Meet Again...

Would you like to find out which of the people around you now you knew in a former life? Prepare to meditate!

Make yourself comfortable. Sit somewhere you can relax. Light a candle if you want or do whatever it is you do to get into that mindset, the one that says you would like to talk to your soul...

Now breathe in on the count of four, hold it for two, breathe out for four and hold it for two. Do that three times.

Now imagine you're in that magical forest. See the trees, feel the air around you, hear the birds, smell the earth... Reach out and touch your forest too.

A path appears before you, a well-trodden path. Go towards it and follow it through the forest.

Keep going deeper into the forest.

Eventually you come to a clearing. In that clearing you will see a very well-tended piece of grass, a circle of impeccable lawn.

At one end is a giant oak tree with what looks like a door in its base. The tree seems to be glowing with light. Its leaves, blowing in the breeze, seem to sing.

You're not going to the tree this time. Instead, make your way to the centre of the lawn, stand there and wait.

In the distance a bell sounds and the door under the tree opens.

Out of the tree come lots of people. Some you may recognize, some may seem oddly familiar but are wearing costumes from another time and place, and some you don't recognize at all.

Look into their eyes as they pass you by and let them form a circle around you.

Now look again, now that they are all there. Look into their eyes and see if you recognize them. Are there any family members there, maybe friends or lovers?

Now all those who have shared a past life with you will stay and the rest will leave. Watch them go.

Who are you left with? Any surprises?

Spend as long as want looking at the people who remain, asking questions of them, gathering information.

When you're ready to leave, bow as a signal you wish to go.

Now see these people leave and return to the base of the tree.

As the door closes behind them, walk back into your forest and along your path back to where you started.

Now let the forest disappear. Let it fade and bring your consciousness back into your room.

Who was there, why and what did they have to say to you?

Tea on, biscuits out – ground yourself and write everything down in case you forget it! It's very important to do this – it may sound as if it's an excuse to eat, but it's really about putting closure on the spiritual and reminding yourself that you live on Earth. Don't be so heavenly minded you're no earthly good!

CHAPTER 7

ANDREW

Some of the most interesting past-life regressions I have done have been with Andrew. He is an entertainer and works very long hours. He travels the country with his manager Sue. We will hear from her later! Andrew lives on the south coast and considers his spirituality to be a work in progress!

Here's how his first regression went:

Andrew

Session One

DW: Tell me what you're wearing on your feet.

A: My legs feel really heavy. I am wearing boots that do up to the knees. There's something like a zip up the legs.

DW: Are you male or female?

A: I am male, I am inside and I have a beard. I have gloves on and a scarf and very dark hair. This place is creaky – not like a boat, more like a beamed house.

DW: What year is it?

A: It's 19-something. It's hard to breathe. I am nervous. I can taste illness, I feel ill and I am in my seventies, or older maybe...

DW: Have a look around you and tell me what you see.

A: Water – lots of water. Outside there's a river and a lock. *[I had to clarify this in case he had said a loch.]* There's a dog nearby, wooden chairs and not much else, to be honest. It's very bare. There's a fireplace with a fire burning and as I look out the window I see the water and fields beyond the lock. It's nice but there's not much there. I am the lock-keeper. I think I have been for ages and ages.

DW: I want you to go back to a time that was important to you. Where do you find yourself?

A: I am in my mid-twenties, there's a big shed and it feels like a farm, but I can't really see it – I feel blocked.

(I sense grief here, a block through grief, but say nothing.)

DW: What's happening now?

A: I am wearing massive boots, really heavy boots, with my trousers tucked into them. My trousers are rough, starchy and very uncomfortable and I am wearing a long waistcoat with thick laces crossing the front to do it up.

I can sense people in the house, cows in the barn and another man at the back of the barn, maybe my dad.

DW: Do you have a family?

A: Mum and dad but no brothers or sisters. I can see my mum. She's wearing a cloth hat, she's a big woman and her essence looks familiar. I think I know her from this life. My dad I also recognize ... I think.

I am shaking, terrified of something, scared someone is going to find me, someone older.

(Andrew is very agitated at this point.)

It's a man, banging on the door, calling me out, arguing with me, but over what...? He is coming in and I recognize him. It's someone I know now, but not very well. He says I have stolen something of his, but I haven't. I don't know what he's talking about.

From nowhere he stabs me – just kills me, stabs me in my left-hand side!

(That was a very sudden departure and a very short life. It seemed that Andrew had actually gone to a different life from that of the lock-keeper. It's been my experience that when the soul delivers such a quick glimpse there's more to come in the light than usual and I wasn't disappointed here.)

DW: Go into the light, Andrew. Surround yourself with it and tell me when you have done that.

A: I am surrounded by it.

DW: Is anyone there to greet you?

A: My mum and dad and some kids and a lady with an odd hat on. A child is speaking and running towards me with daisies, then skipping away.

I see my murderer, I recognize him, and he is telling me it was all a misunderstanding. Someone had said I had stolen his stuff. He says he shouldn't have listened to gossip and he's sorry.

My guide is there – at least I think it's my guide.

DW: Can you describe him?

A: He is tall. I'm not sure now if it's a he or a she. There's silver-grey light. My guide is kissing me on the right cheek. I can see stars, lots of stars.

No, he's not my guide, he's a parent. He says, 'I love you.' He touches the back of my neck to show when he's around.

(Andrew is silent for while here and is left to his thoughts.)

DW: So now tell me what negative thing you want to release from that life.

A: A feeling of fear, fear of fear itself.

DW: And what positive thing do you want to bring back with you?

A: It was a simple life. I want a simple life.

This may seem like a very simple and not that exciting regression, but Andrew had just had confirmation that he was a Star Child – a child who has incarnated to show us all how simple life can be when we try, how easy it can be if you simply let go, enjoy life and live every moment to the full, which I have to say Andrew does. Star Children are often not that great with earthly things, which may be why his manager and very good friend is a Taurus – an earth sign and a very practical one at that!

I asked Andrew if he had a birthmark where he was stabbed in that life, and once he got over the surprise, he admitted that he had.

This first regression intrigued me. I have only ever regressed one other Star Child and I find the concept fascinating. Can there really be children born into human bodies whose heritage is among the stars? It seemed to me from what I saw when I travelled with Andrew in that life that it really could be the case – his Star Father even gave me a message that was something nobody knew, least of all Andrew himself.

Andrew's regression served to remind me that just when you think you've seen everything, you realize you know nothing at all... I had to ask him back.

Andrew

Session Two

DW: What are you wearing on your feet?

A: Nothing. I have bare feet.

DW: Are you inside or outside?

A: Outside. It's hot, a desert. It's a long time ago. I'm male. I'm happy being alone.

DW: What's happening now?

A: I can see tents, people packing things away. I'm just walking while they are packing. I'm wearing something plain, lighter than hessian but that sort of thing, with a brown belt and a gold-studded leather wristband and I think I have something on my head. I also think I have earrings. My hair's not long – above my ears, just above.

DW: What country is this?

A: Egypt.

DW: What is your name?

(Andrew tries to give his name in Egyptian. His voice changes, which is a rare event in my experience.)

A: It's Hem, Hemiel, something like that.

DW: Tell me what's happening now.

A: As I walk, there are loads of people moving somewhere. I don't know why. The sun is flickering. We're travelling somewhere important and taking a long time moving something. It's important. It's not something heavy. It's a box. There's something in there. The box itself is wooden, a light-coloured box, nothing special.

DW: What's in there?

A: Something to do with the sun.

DW: Where are you now?

A: Night-time or underground. It's all very still. There's a huge rock to my left, a great rock in the desert. We're at the bottom of it. People are sleeping. It smells a bit. It's an important place to stop at. There are other people there who are going somewhere else.

There are flickering lights up high. I don't know where. There's a sound – something escaping, animals maybe. Something's charging – *no*, it's an ambush! Animals are being released like a stampede – huge hairy things, huge like bulls. There's panic, everyone is shouting. I'm running. There's a sword – I don't know where it's coming from – going into the animals.

There are hundreds of people and only a few of us. They want what's in the box.

(Andrew is very animated at this point.)

We're going, heading towards a sea of people. I don't know what is in this box. We're close to a mountain. There's a sea of people cutting and cutting and cutting.

(At this point I begin to rub my neck as it feels sore, a warning from my guides that Andrew is about to lose his head, perhaps?)

It's OK.

(Andrew begins laughing, which doesn't seem in keeping with events.)

That's it – a really big man hit my neck and took my head off.

DW: Go into the light, Andrew, and tell me when you're completely surrounded by it.

A: They chopped me up into bits. They carried them away, put them on spikes and decorated swords and things with them. I don't feel anything.

There's a woman there in the light. She's big and she's nice, but doesn't look it. Her name – I can hear it but don't understand it. Three something – Third Dynasty perhaps? She speaks through her body. She has a noise, a song perhaps. No – she says no like a constant noise. She's a statue, but she's not. I don't think she's real. I feel sort of, sort of floaty.

DW: What was in the box?

A: A pot with something in it. There was writing on it, a scroll with marks on, an alphabet. It was written by the woman. It was something about the sun, her and the sun. The writing was a key, a code, something that made sense of what had been written. The people wanted to take it but not use it. They really didn't like it.

DW: Is there anyone else there with you?

A: Doors are opening... I can see something. Time has stopped. It's almost as though I'm not breathing. It's all really bright. I hold out my hand and it's just white. I can't describe it really. It's really fast but not. There are colours but not. It's as though I'm on a path and no one else is. Things are moving around – flick, flick, flick. If you look there's nothing there, but if you stare something appears.

Now the archangel Michael, with huge hands, is facing my right-hand side. It's as though he's holding my hand. My whole body is shaking with the high power. He's saying, 'Listen.'

Something is blocking my way. He's sealed it – for the time being.

He's getting bigger. I'm sitting in his hand – he's lifted me up in his right hand, put me up by his head. Now I'm looking at it – but I don't know what I'm looking at. There are rays of light. It's warm. There's something like a cage to my left.

DW: What negative traits do you want to leave behind?

A: Being cruel, nasty and aggressive.

DW: And what are the positive ones you want to bring forward?

A: Being confident and carefree.

There's more to Andrew's regression than is obvious at first. The life is likely to have been one as a priest/ protector of sacred artefacts, but his connection to those artefacts was deeper than first appears.

Was the female he encountered in the light a real being or a reflection of a higher force? Perhaps Andrew was being given a connection to something within himself, something that with some effort he could bring to the fore to help him lead a more magical life in the here and now.

The time he talks of is full of mystery and there's a part of me that thinks it was actually a simpler time that enabled many to have a stronger connection the higher realms than we have now, thanks to modern distractions.

Making space to be alone, to find time to open that line of communication, would be very good for Andrew and incorporating images from that time into his meditations might unlock more.

Andrew is obviously on a very strongly guided path and the appearance of the archangel Michael in his regression only served to reinforce that.

Andrew has decided to wait a while before having another regression, but meantime continues his path, attending workshops and weekend events when he can. His own comments were as follows:

When David first asked me to sit for a past-life regression I was a little apprehensive, but at the same time very excited. We began with no high expectations and I have to say the first part of my regression seemed very boring, mundane and sluggish, with not a lot happening at all. 'Excellent,' I thought, 'a normal life. This must be real!'

I have a very active imagination and I was a little worried that I might conjure up someone I had heard or read about, but this was not the case. Thank heavens I didn't regress into Caesar or Cleopatra!

The sensation of the regression is one that will stay with me always. It was very insular and private while at the same time I was acutely aware of it taking place in the here and now. Being in two places at the same time was certainly an eye-opener.

During my first session I was surprised to find my body actually reacting to what was happening. I was physically shaking when I was afraid and struggling for breath as I grew older – a strange experience that wasn't overly comfortable but was confir-mation to me that I was there.

At the end of this session I found the 'moving to the light' section to be the most amazing thing I have ever encountered and this was where I felt I became more detached from the here and now. A beautiful place became clear to me, with breathtaking images. I saw those images as clearly as I see the world outside my window now. It was a truly life-changing and deeply personal experience that I am glad to have shared with David.

I looked into Star Children, as David had mentioned them to me after the first regres-sion, and me being me, I had to rush out and buy a book instantly on the subject. While reading the book I was amazed, as I felt it described me many, many times, Coinci-dence? I'm not sure, but what a great jour-ney of discovery lies ahead.

My second regression was more vivid than the first. Maybe this was because I had done it before, so I was more relaxed and could visualize 'getting there' more easily. As you have read, I 'landed' in a desert I knew to be Egypt and everything seemed to happen at great speed. I knew exactly who I was and what I was doing – I had a purpose, it seemed.

I had seen documentaries on Egypt, but did not have any previous knowledge about anything from my regression. Afterwards I spoke to a friend who said that people used to put stones in pots with scrolls to act as keys to deciphering the texts. I'm not sure if this is true, but it's worth further investigation.

The strange thing was the feeling when I had been killed – there was nothing! Looking at the dismemberment of my physical body, I wasn't distressed or upset. I knew that that life was over and I was safe in the light. Being in the light was another eye-opener! I felt very calm and serene, more happened spiritually than I ever expected and it seemed to point me in a direction, which we all need at some point in our lives, I think.

I will follow up on both past-life regressions and try to make sense of them personally. However for me the best part was being in the light, a magical place where time stood still... It was simple, beautiful, personal and life-changing.

Thank you.

CHAPTER 8

ONCE IS ENOUGH?

Andrew had a couple of regressions, but here are some past lives from people who have come to me for just one – at least so far! Some people may only have one regression in their life and that's it for any structured investigation. Maybe once is enough to let them know they have been here before. If they don't go further, that doesn't mean they aren't on a spiritual path, though. I personally believe we are all on a spiritual path and I am horrified when I hear people big themselves up by saying they are on 'the path' as if they are somehow something special. The truth is we all travel that road. Aren't we all spiritual beings trying to be human?

Let's look at the path a few people have taken through the ages...

Sue

Sue is Andrew's manager. She lives in the south and before this regression she had had no experience at all of meditation or any spiritually-led practices such as past-life regression. She is single and a very earthy Taurus!

DW: Tell me when you have landed.

S: OK. I have landed, I think.

DW: What are you wearing on your feet?

S: Nothing. There's something wrong with my feet. I can't figure it out yet.

DW: Are you inside or out?

S: It's dark. I'm outside. There are trees – two lots of trees. Feet – has a – *[can't quite get it out here]*.

DW: What are you wearing?

S: It feels like a really rough dress. I have bad knees, soaking hair, not tied up – it's short hair, straggling. I'm female, aged 20, 22. I have very clear skin, but I'm poorly, not well. My hair colour is brown, but it's dirty. I'm not very tall – 5 ft 2 inches-ish.

DW: What's happening now?

S: I'm outside. It's still dark. It feels like I'm hiding in a bank by trees. Hiding from someone?

DW: Go back to a time that's significant for you, Sue.

S: I can see round huts made of logs. Inside each hut there's lots of smoke. Inside there are people; outside it's very dark. I think it's in Surrey. I am being told I can't go anywhere, I must stay where I am. Someone older has said I can't go out. Last time I went out was months ago and I got into trouble. Later on a man, a horrible man, beat me. He said I deserved it. Now I'm cowering in a corner and he's shouting. He doesn't know what he's saying. I'm very scared. I can't get out – don't know how to.

DW: Is there anyone else around you?

S: Only him. It's dark. Legs – weedy. Bruises – arms, bruises. Burnt on left arm a long time ago.

DW: What do you do about it?

S: I'm running into the forest, into the woods. Nobody sees me. Nobody could have seen me.

Now it's the morning. I'm scared that he will find me. I didn't think it though. I am in the trees, in the wind. There are no birds. Nobody comes. I'm trying to move on. I don't think anybody followed me, but I don't care – just need to get away.

Walking through the woods. It's bright and blue now. Nobody's coming after me. I am at the edge of the forest. It's really blue and bright. There's a field. There's nobody there, just a field. I don't know where I'm going, but don't feel scared. There are yellow flowers there, bright yellow flowers. They are so lovely.

DW: What happens next, Sue?

S: I am in a house in a bed. Someone is there, a woman, older, about 40. She's looking after me. My legs are wrong. I've just not recovered from being confined at home all this time.

DW: Do you recognize this woman?

S: No. She's looking after me, but I die. I was taken in. She's my sister in this life, because she is older. I can't understand why she found me, took me in.

DW: Go into the light, Sue, tell me what you see.

S: I can see my guide in a long brown coat. He's male, 19 or 20, young, handsome, looks sad.

DW: Why would he be looking sad?

S: I think he's just solemn, very serious.

DW: What is he saying to you?

S: 'You need to work at it.' My guide stands up, says I shouldn't be scared, should run in this life too!

DW: What negative thing do you want to leave behind?

S: Being scared.

DW: What positive trait do you want to bring back with you?

S: Taking action and being courageous.

Sue's experience was interesting. Her guide summed it all up perfectly and as I write this an interview on the radio with an entrepreneur is coming to an end – he has summed up his success by saying, 'Just get off your backside and do it!' What synchronicity. Wish Sue had heard it!

Often people experience lives where they are held against their will. Not all escape, but the message is usually the same: you need to get out and show yourself to the world and let it show itself to you. If you experience these lives, think about how you can make your world bigger and ultimately better.

Sue's regression also proves you don't have to have done this sort of work before to gain remarkable results and even an earthy Taurus can lift themselves up into the realms of astral travel!

Sue herself commented:

Afterwards I realized that the lady in that life that I thought was my sister was in fact my mum. I felt odd seeing her. She has been dead for 18 years, so it was very emotional.

I also think my name was something like Oriel, something like that. That came as I was writing out my regression as David had suggested.

I'd just gone along to support Andrew and past-life regression wasn't something I would have done if it hadn't been David doing it, but I am glad I did. I wasn't sure how it could benefit you in this life, but now I am trying to be more courageous and true to myself. I speak my mind a lot more rather than going with the flow.

It has also made me more open-minded about it all. It's actually one of the most bizarre things I have ever done, but it felt as if it was so real! I saw, heard, felt, touched that other life... It was nothing like I expected at all, but I am glad I did it and would definitely do it again.

Someone else who came to support a friend and did not really intend to have a regression herself was Jill...

Jill

Jill is a garden designer – a great job for a Taurus! She lives in Oxfordshire and has her own business. When she came to me she was about to put a garden into the world-famous Hampton Court flower show and it was themed around spirit.

DW: What are you wearing on your feet?

J: Leather sandals covered with dust. It's everywhere, all over me. I'm a man and really, really fit. I have a spear in my hands and I'm wearing a helmet with flaps on it, made of leather and metal. The spear is made of wood with a metal tip.

DW: Where are you?

J: Hot, home. Greece, I think.

DW: Is there anyone with you?

J: Yes, there are people around, crowds making a noise, shouting, being aggressive and watching.

DW: Watching what?

J: A building. That looks like a gladiator. It's an arena. There are lots of people. They are not criminals, they want to be here. I am waiting to go on, into the arena, I am riding a horse and carrying a spear.

DW: When is this?

J: Early – 211, I think. There's a lot of dust. It's horrible, hot horses' dust. But it's not aggressive, there's not fighting or racing.

Afterwards, after the show, I'm in a place where lots of men are sitting around with women serving. Loads of them are eating. There's leather, white robes, a tall ceiling. It's a barracks – very grand.

There's a 'P' in my name.

Water, channels of water through a garden – I'm walking in a garden, touching the water. It looks so beautiful.

DW: Go to a time that's important to you, Jill.

J: I'm walking through streets. I'm about 40. It's night. I have sand in my hair. It's dusty. There are palm trees, smells... I don't like it, don't like the dust.

(Jill feels uncomfortable physically. Her neck and face go red at this point.)

DW: What's happening now? What are you seeing or thinking?

J: He is a grand man, very grand, a general, smelling like dirt now and again, but with so many clothes.

DW: Where are you now?

J: At a table with people, loads of men, sitting beneath me. There are three tables, with cloths and gold cups. This is home. There are two other people there, not family. I have a family, but they're not important. My wife has long hair. It's beautiful, she has a ribbon in her hair. They are seven and nine, the kids, boy and a girl, and the girl is younger, but they are not so important now. The job and power are more important to me.

I know the emperor, but don't know who he is.

(I do – it's Jill herself!)

DW: What's happening now?

J: I am dead. I see a person sitting beside a huge coffin with a lid. I died of old age, aged 60-something. Died of old age. The person sitting by the coffin is my wife. She speaks. I hurt her but she loves me. I didn't care enough. I was happy because I'd done my own thing.

Two small children are there holding hands.

I can see my guide. She's wearing pale green velvet. Agneta, Agnes – her name's something like that.

DW: What negative traits do you want to leave behind?

J: I hurt a lot of people.

DW: What do you want to bring back into this life?

J: Power is good. Leadership, confidence – I would like more of that.

Here's an email Jill sent to me a few days later:

David,

Thank you so much for the extraordinary day yesterday. The one thing I could not bring myself to say during the regression (although I told Tessa on the way home) was when you asked me who the emperor was, I wanted to say 'Me!', but it sounded so immodest and frankly ridiculous.

I am stunned. I have just been on the Internet and keyed in 'Roman life AD 211'. It seems Emperor Septimius Severus died peacefully in AD 211 in York, England, aged 64. He was born in AD 146 in Lepcis Magna in Libya, which had the largest coliseum outside Rome in the world. The Hadrianic Baths were the most splendid monument in Lepcis and were finished in AD 137.

Severus started his army career as a foot soldier and rose through the ranks. He was deployed at York to protect the empire against invasion by the Scots at Hadrian's Wall. He did indeed have the figure of a god!

He married, but his first wife died after ten years, having borne him no children. His second wife was very beautiful and bore him two sons (not a son and a daughter, as I thought).

He loved cooking [a talent Jill has carried through]. *His legacies were the changes he made to the Roman army, allowing married officers to live with their wives and increasing their pay by half.*

The Internet pictures and images are so similar to the ones in my mind, it may as well be the very place I saw.

No more words left...

Jill

Jill's regression showed her that she was capable, more capable than she had thought, but her research after the regression answered a more far-reaching question: had she lived before?

Her friend's regression also brought questions and answers...

Tessa

Tessa runs her own business from her ever-present BlackBerry! She lives near Oxford. She came to see me because she was haunted by a face in her meditations and sometimes when she went to sleep, and she wondered if it was a link to a past life.

DW: Tell me when you have landed, Tessa, and what you're wearing on your feet.

T: I have landed and I am wearing sandals. I'm outside, in a forest. I feel old and very cold! I am a male, fiftyish, European. Am I in England? I am living in a forest. I see grey sky. My beard is red and scruffy and I know I don't know many people. I have no family.

DW: What's happening now?

T: I am eating, eating anything I can – berries and rabbits. Something happened in the past.

DW: We will get to that, what year is it?

(Tessa jumps back in time here. Finding out what happened in the past needed no further prompts from me, then!)

T: It's 1488. I am six years old. I'm in a cottage, playing with sticks. I can hear a man and a woman talking. I am listening. They are not happy.

DW: Why?

T: I don't understand. We've not got much; we're always hungry. Dad – he came to the house. Mum, she's wearing brown, a dirty dress and a bonnet.

Looking at the house, it's made of wood. There are logs outside the porch and door. There's no glass in the windows. There's a fire in the room, a chimney in the middle. It's smoky...

There's just me there now. I'm seven years old now. I don't know where they have gone. Where have they gone...?

DW: Move forwards to a time that's important, Tessa.

T: I am 14. The townspeople are jabbing at me, poking fun at me. I don't know what happened to Mum and Dad...

DW: Where are you now?

T: I am about 55. I'm walking to a river. It's cold. I drop in. It's taking me away. I'm peaceful, coming away from my head...

DW: Go into the light and tell me what happened.

T: I drowned.

DW: Is there anyone there?

T: My guide is there. His eyes are big. He's saying he's here to help me, wants to develop my spiritual side more. Tiga is his name, I think. He smiles at me and says hello to you. He touches me on the arm as a sign that he's around, a sign for future visits.

DW: What negative things do you want to leave behind from that life?

T: Not knowing what happened. Needing to know.

DW: What positive things do you want to bring back with you?

T: How much Mum loved me. It wasn't very positive a life really, but she did love me.

Tessa's face in the night may have been the image of her mother looking for her. Or perhaps it showed an inner knowledge that over the centuries we can find other people and make sure we are in each other's lives.

Here's what Tessa wrote after her experience:

David,

Thank you so much for all your help and support on Tuesday. It was a fantastic experience which has made a huge impact on me – far more than I realized on the day.

You said to write everything down and more would come – it certainly did. Questions also came up that I wanted to ask of you – I hope you can help me answer them! There are some bits which I have questioned, as I think I didn't always answer you as fully as I could have done. I think it was a bit of self-protection!

If it helps in your understanding of the story and should you wish to use it in future writing, then I think the lesson to be learned is that you cannot isolate yourself and protect yourself happily all your life. Today I am very independent and can be very self-sufficient, which hasn't always made my close relationships easy. I think that needs addressing.

I also have a difficult relationship with my mother which I cannot solve. I will use this to progress that further!

I also wanted to let you know that I slept well on Tuesday and I have been visited again but with a smile and a touch, which wasn't spooky but very comforting!

Tessa

As you can see, Tessa's interpretation of events is what matters. She did the right thing by recording her experience afterwards in her own words and even though some of the information has been difficult for her, it has brought greater understanding to the here and now – which is the point!

CHAPTER 9

FORGIVENESS

One of the most difficult lessons past-life regressions can present us with is that of forgiveness – which is also why it's so rewarding, of course!

This past life was sent to me by Jacy, who lives in Australia:

I would like to share with you one of my past lives that I recall in great detail. From the age of four or five, I used to draw a large red barn or farmhouse like one you would find in America. I remember very distinctly being given permission by a teacher one day in kindergarten to draw on the blackboard with coloured chalks, because all the teachers loved to watch me draw and encouraged my gift. For some reason, I was compelled to draw this red barn.

As I grew up, I often dreamed of floating over this barn. I often woke feeling sad and with a deep longing to return to that farm. It wasn't until the age of 18, when I was passing an old Victorian Gothic-style home on my way to university, that further details of that life were triggered. Around that time I dreamed I was a man in his early sixties living at the turn of the century. I appeared to be very rich and lived in a large home with what looked like Gothic-style architecture – the type you would see in many parts of America. In my dream I was watching the man as though I was out of my body, yet I knew the man was me. I was in my drawing room when suddenly two men burst into the house. A scuffle broke out; I was shot and hit on the head. I was suddenly floating above my body and could see my head injury and the pool of blood I was lying in. In front of my eyes, I then saw a newspaper article with the headline that I had been murdered and robbed in my own home. I assumed I was a very influential man.

Being young and not knowing much about past lives, I had no idea what to make of this dream. I couldn't talk to anyone about it, but I just knew that what I had seen had been me and while at the time I was still unsure about the nature of our existence, I knew this mystery would unfold.

A few years later, in 1997, I remember having a very vivid dream of my entire family living in another country in another time. My father, mother, sister, younger brother and I were all men in a family of bandits or looters! The terrain looked like Mediterranean. It had many castles that had been built during the crusades. At the time I did not know the historical details of that area, but since then I have discovered that that was highly possible.

The dream began with my father leading us into a castle which we were to loot (my father appeared to be the head of our gang of looters). I felt the personalities of my mother, brother and sister in that lifetime very strongly. I felt their greed and excitement, whereas I was feeling great trepidation, guilt and fear for the safety of my father.

He told us to stay behind while he checked if the coast was clear. I recall him ascending some stone stairs and drawing a sword. I cried out for him to stop and my mother (the second in command) said, 'Leave him!

Let's take these things and go.' The others were all gathering pieces from the castle, anything they could carry, and had greed in their eyes.

I could hear a distant sword fight and somehow knew it was with some knights who held shields with red crosses. Then one chased my father down the stairs, with his sword drawn. I called out, 'No!' but the knight stabbed my father before my eyes in the right-hand side of his chest below his ribcage.

My father yelled out, 'Leave! Save yourselves!'

I was dragged out screaming by the rest of my family/the bandits. We got away and the dream ended.

A couple of months later my father complained of a persistent pain on his right side under his ribcage. They discovered it was gallstones and he needed an operation to remove them. But after their removal, as he lay in the hospital bed he continued to complain of 'stabbing pains' in that area of his body. The pathology results showed that he actually had a very rare and aggressive cancer of the gallbladder. It had spread to his liver and within three months, much to our grief and shock, he passed away.

I still believe that the dream I had of the crusades actually occurred. I believe that wound left a type of 'memory' in my father's physical body and that somehow in this life part of the healing we all needed was of the guilt that we left him behind hundreds of years ago.

Since that dream, I've been very interested in the possibilities of past lives. In 2002 I began to discover my clairaudient/clairvoyant abilities. I found I was able to hear my angels and spirit guides and write down what they said. They would literally 'dictate' to me paragraphs of information about spiritual truths as well as personal information and details for my own personal growth.

One evening they asked me to meditate while they revealed to me the truth about one of my past lives. Like a movie running before my eyes, I saw in the greatest detail my life as a poor Irish immigrant in Texas during the mid-1800s. My family had immigrated there for a better life and I was only a young boy when we arrived. I was shown that my father had left us when we arrived and my mother had several children to look after, with no source of income.

A kind man who befriended our family allowed us to live in a farmhouse on a small patch of land and asked if he could take me under his wing and teach me to tend to cattle. I worked extremely hard and was able to provide some income for my mother and brothers and sisters. I began to grow increasingly clever in not only the rustling of cattle but also the sale of cattle and livestock.

Very soon, my wealth began to grow and I was able to buy a patch of land. As fortune goes, luck was on my side: on this patch of land, I struck oil! This led to a huge influx of wealth for me and tremendous life change for my family. But, remembering my poor roots, I felt that the town we lived in needed much in the way of development. I began to lobby the council to build more roads, a proper school, hotels and such.

I was told that in that life they called me 'Junior', but since then I have felt through meditation that my surname may have been Corbett and the first name may have been William.

In my new life as a rich man, I had to hire servants and I aimed to help many Irish immigrants. One of my favourite servants was a young Irish lady whom I seemed to be very attracted to. (I have since discovered that my partner of three years was that maid.)

One day when I was riding my horse out in my cornfield, I saw a young teenage girl stealing food from the field. I was amused and called out to her. She didn't move but continued to gather some of my corn. I rode up closer and called again, and again she didn't hear me. I moved closer and grabbed her around the waist and pulled her up onto my horse! She screamed out and at that moment I realized she was deaf!

She was very dirty and had no shoes on. She tried to hit me over the head with the corn and I simply laughed and rode back to my house and ordered the servants to clean her and dress her in new clothes. My Irish maid was not impressed! But she did as she was told.

I discovered through much effort that the woman's name was Daisy and that she and her younger brothers were orphans. (She was, I felt, a man I was having a relation-

ship with at that time – a brief but important karmic and emotional connection.) She was attempting to avoid being put back into the orphanage by hiding out and stealing food. She was only 15 at the time and the law stated that she needed to be returned to the orphanage along with her brothers. When I saw the state of the institution I was appalled and made great efforts to have new premises built for the orphans.

It felt as though I constantly wished to help the poor in the town and better the community. For a great many people this was a wonderful thing, but I had my enemies, who envied my position.

I kept in regular contact with Daisy and had her learn a form of sign language so that she could function better in day-to-day life. When she turned 17, I was able to remove her from the orphanage legally, and I married her.

Many townsfolk were shocked, as a local mayor had been pushing for me to marry his daughter. We were happy, but many people were not, especially my Irish maid, Moira. She stood by my side, but did not approve of my choice of bride.

Shortly after our marriage, Daisy gave birth to our son, but six months afterwards she was taken ill with a disease of the lungs. It may have been a disease related to a childhood illness that flares up later in life – I'm not sure, but that was the feeling. In those days it was simply called 'a fever'. One night in bed Daisy woke up coughing violently and she died shortly after.

The trauma of losing her resulted in my becoming a recluse. I could barely care for my son and Moira seemed to take over the role of caregiver. I never remarried, but it seems that Moira and I had an unconventional 'marriage' of sorts behind closed doors. Although we loved each other, I never revealed our relationship to anyone and she deeply resented the fact that I would not marry her. In many meditations since then, I have uncovered the nature of my relationship with Moira and have seen some patterns emerge in my current life with my partner. I feel there is a resistance in both of us to 'properly tie the knot'.

Once, during a meditation, I asked for greater clarity on what happened to Moira after my murder and needless to say I saw her mortification and grief, but also saw my funeral, as though I was floating by it. It appears Moira was left most of my wealth and she continued to care for my son.

This appears to be extremely detailed and many may say that it is just the result of an overactive imagination. But I can tell you that the story I am relaying here has been pieced together over many dreams and meditations.

The patterns and lessons I can see in my life now. For example, up until a couple of years ago I had a deep fear of being rich and often felt as though it was wrong. I feel that may have carried over from the fact that I was murdered for my status and wealth in that lifetime.

I often guide myself through various meditations and pose questions about some of the past lives I can recall, asking for healing in some areas of my life. I sometimes ask about current ailments and ask for the source. Images often appear of past lives showing me injuries, etc., in the area of the illness.

I have even recalled another life in the late 1700s where I was the maid of a duke who was having an affair with me but he wouldn't go against his family and 'marry down' and instead told me he was marrying a woman of rank of whom his father approved.

After seeing that lifetime in dreams over the years, with the same emotional argument where the duke wouldn't take me as his wife, I decided recently to meditate on it and make peace with that lifetime. I saw the scene before me and instead of allowing myself to react emotionally and beg for him to stay with me, I told him, 'I release you and respect you for your decision. I cannot expect you to go against your family and I understand your decision and why you have made it. You have my total blessing to go on with your life and have a happy marriage.'

When I said that, it was almost as if the duke (another ex-boyfriend in this lifetime for me) had a cloud lift from his face. I, too, felt lighter, as if I had released a heavy burden and deep resentment. It was truly remarkable!

Who knows what sort of impact that visualization of making peace might have had on my ex-boyfriend? I will never know. At our last contact, about four years ago, I learned he had entered into an arranged marriage and was deeply unhappy. Perhaps there are better days ahead for him.

What a lifetime of past-life memories from Jacy! The interesting thing is that she has used a combination of dream analysis and meditation to uncover her journey and has recognized various key relationships along the way. It seems as if she acts upon what she sees and that's so important. Information is given to each of us to do something with. Failure to do that turns what has come from your soul into nothing more than interesting dinner-party conversation.

Jacy has also brought a skill through from a former life – her ability to draw – and coupled with her abilities as a seer, it's clearly working well for her, as is her recognition of patterns and habits from past lives. When you uncover your own, perhaps using some of the techniques here or in my previous book, *Past, Present and Future*, be sure to look for your own patterns and the gifts you have brought through – and what you would like to leave behind, of course.

Jacy also went back into a former life and made peace with a character from her past. Though she's not sure what the effect has been on the person in this incarnation, when this is done with love – and it should always be done with love – nothing but good can come from it.

If you'd like to try it, here's a technique to help you:

- Imagine the person from your past life is in front of you.

- See them surrounded in a bubble of pink light.

- Let that light completely surround them and start to move through them, flooding them in healing and forgiving light.

- Surround the pink light with a band of silver and see it float off into the past to send healing back to a time when things might not have been so good.

- Now let it go and trust in its effect.

Miracles may not happen but subtle changes can make all the difference and if you're looking for them, they will show themselves. I have done this and it has made some situations a whole lot easier!

CHAPTER 10

THE AFTERLIFE

One question that people often ask is: can we glimpse the afterlife through past-life regression? Some people want to see what life is like *between* lives – what it's like in heaven, effectively.

Sometimes clients do go into the astral worlds during a regression – they see what it's like on the other side, if you like. You have already seen some of that in some of the stories so far. I have to say, though, that no one has yet reported growing wings and sitting around on clouds playing a harp! Life in the other side of the veil seems to be similar to this: work to be done, things to learn, healing to take place...

Here's a life, sent to me by Bulldog, that led towards and into the light...

I am married with one child. In 1985 I was regressed by a hypnotherapist at my home in Upper Norwood, on the outskirts of London. The session took place in my living room. Both the hypnotherapist and I had a tape recorder. He was sitting on the settee with a large notepad and pen.

I could feel hot sand under my feet. When I looked down I could see my feet were bare and I had skinny little legs. I was wearing some kind of tunic tied round my waist with a piece of cloth. I felt like a boy and for some reason knew I was about seven to eight years of age. I could hear a voice shouting at me and others to move and I knew one of the voices was that of my father. I also knew a lot of the men that were busy working in the heat hauling gigantic cut stones about.

Suddenly everything went black as a stone fell on top of me. I felt my chest feel very heavy, then nothing more. I don't know the date or what my name was, as it all happened so fast.

Next I was a young girl standing outside a muddy campsite and there were men sitting and standing around drinking and having what sounded like a good time. It was very noisy and I felt quite sad, as there were also women there who were laughing and having fun with these men. Some were cuddling them and sitting on their laps and some were dancing with them. A lot of the men had long bushy hair and beards. One of these women was my mother and I knew she wasn't enjoying herself.

As I looked around, there were shovels and metal pans lying around. Animal skins were hanging up outside the tents. The tents themselves were of a dark material not unlike the green tents of the 1950s. There were horses pulling large wooden open boxes on wheels. Everyone was pleased the rain had stopped.

I knew my name was Annie and I was half-Indian. My mother was an Indian.

The next I remember I was standing in the open. The dry grass under my feet was scorched from the sun. I was watching a trail of woman and children I knew walking in a long line moving to somewhere safer. I could sense the desperateness of the journey.

At this point I felt I was in my thirties and knew it was the 1800s. I felt sad and thought about my father. His name was John Fitzgerald. I remembered him walk-

ing off into the distance in a worn thick two-piece jacket and trousers. Over his shoulder he carried a very large satchel made from animal skin. I was not sure why or when he left, but knew he had to leave. I remembered standing watching him until I couldn't see him anymore.

Next I found myself in an attic room. The year was 1870. I felt I was around 81 or 82 years of age. The roof was apex-shaped with a tiny window in the middle of the apex and the sun was filtering through in a line across the wooden floor. I had a little low-down bed made from wood: nothing fancy, just basic. The rest of the room was very dark.

Someone came up to the attic, opened the door, put a plate of food on the floor and then left, shutting the door behind her. Her skirt was quite full and her hair was half-up and half-down. For some reason she didn't speak and didn't show me any kindness, but I knew her and I knew she was cruel to me and had always been embarrassed by my presence.

I could hear talking downstairs. My body felt so tired and I lay down on my bed. I felt the end would come soon.

I felt throughout this session that I was an onlooker, experiencing the lives again from a safe distance but with the knowledge of who I was and how I felt.

Some things now are going to be extremely hard to explain, but I will try my best. You will have to form your own opinions. If you don't believe this happened to me, then that's fine too. Maybe it will be good to share and just get it off my chest.

There was an experiment I felt I needed to do, so I talked the hypnotherapist into it and eventually he agreed to regress me to just after Annie died, although he was very unsure about what would happen or even if it would work.

I hasten to say that it did work and to this day I cannot do anything but believe what I experienced. I am now 54 years of age and slowly through the years things have started making sense. It's almost like piecing a jigsaw together, but when you think you are near to seeing the picture, more pieces appear.

The hypnotherapist took me back to 1870, when Annie was in the attic. She was just at the point of dying. He skipped the actual death and asked me where I was.

For me, the whole side of the apex where the little window was had completely gone, the light was so bright. This light began to turn into a white cloudy mixture with pale hues of colour swirling slowly. Through this cloudy substance came a figure I knew. His name was White Owl. He looked so beautiful. He wrapped his arms around me and I felt enveloped in a feeling of security.

We started to rise upwards through the cloud. I cannot describe the feeling – it was something I had never felt before. I then remember everything going slightly dark and I felt as though I was turning in a spiral and then had a sinking feeling that was strange but not unpleasant. Then a nothingness came over me.

Then I was in a field of the plushest, softest grass I have ever felt and in the distance I could see a massive domed building held up by columns. It was very gently pulsating, as if it was breathing. It was luminous and I could see straight through it as if it were a piece of glass. I knew I had to get there but didn't know how, as I couldn't seem to walk.

I eventually found I could glide there with thoughts. The closer I got, the smaller the building seemed. When I arrived by the steps, someone came out from behind one of the columns. I could tell he was male by his face, but he had no legs. His body seemed to tail off and he was almost transparent. He introduced himself and told me they had been expecting me and that he would take me into the hall of learning.

Inside the building it was like the TARDIS – it just went on and on. It was enormous. There were others like my host and I could only tell who was male or female by the faces, as there was no shape to the bodies that would give away the sex. At that point I decided to look down at myself and realized I didn't have any feet or legs either. I felt as if I was floating. My host turned to me and, without speaking, explained that without a body we could not be sexed; we were neither male nor female.

I started feeling a bit strange but at home. My host then told me I would need to rest a while so I could – dare I say it? – pulse in the same rhythm.

Before I was taken to rest my host told me I was to meet the administering council, the higher beings who were very learned. I didn't really understand.

Then I heard a voice asking me where I was and I said, 'Leave me alone.'

Next I was resting on a sort of soft platform and another male was swirling colours around me. I began to feel more relaxed and comfortable and must have drifted off.

The host came for me again and we went through into another area. I will cut to the nitty-gritty here, otherwise it will take me forever to type! I was shown what we really look like and the only way I can describe it is that we look like bubbles. [Could this be our aura?] *The Earth was shown to me and I was told our platform was unstable. I could see large black patches where minerals, metals and rocks had been removed and waste products had been deposited instead. This meant that our filter system had been destroyed, and other things too.*

I was allowed to ask questions but was told I would only be allowed to receive answers up to the level of understanding I had reached.

Birth, death, knowledge – this is what the council was able to show me and tell me. I learned that there is no beginning and no end, life is a never-ending circle of knowledge and experiences which helps us to move higher. There are so many different levels, level upon level. Nobody can go up from the level they are on until they are ready. Birth is a sad occasion; death is a joyful occasion.

We do not speak to a god, we are in tune with our higher self, and we are from one source but split into millions. To explain this, I was shown a picture of a large circle with lines going off in all directions from it and another circle on the end of each line and two lines going off the circles and circles off these lines and so on. The main circle is the whole thing. Let's call it the mother. Part of the mother is split into smaller circles and they are split again and again. Each split is still part of the mother but on different levels. Each time we earn knowledge and gain experiences, these are transferred back to the mother, but that doesn't necessarily mean we have finished with a particular level.

When I asked who or what God was, quite a stern voice told me G.O.D. was an acronym of Genocide Over Detriment. It said we were not just happy harming everything we touched but we wanted to kill everything, which made it more difficult for us to move onwards and upwards.

I asked about what happened to people who died and was very surprised by some of the answers, but it made sense. When the life of the body we inhabit starts to die, it cannot sustain us any more, just like a house that's falling down, so we have no choice but to vacate it.

I asked what the council thought about the cruelty of people being kept in pain and alive in old bodies. They said that other species on Earth killed their young and old because they knew the body they were in could not function and realized that they would only suffer, but we hadn't yet learned the lesson of release. I was told in so many words that we could learn a lot from the smaller species.

Amongst other things they also told me I was an observer in my life now. It was a bit of a shock going there from Annie and then being bought up to date.

I asked about people here who seem be able to come up with things that are out of this world, giving the example of Leonardo da Vinci. The answer was that he had lived before with the knowledge of flying and had returned to a simpler way of life for another experience.

I was also told we all have abilities – music, art, laughter, listening – but others often stop us from fulfilling these individual talents. This leads to disaster in many of us and many people do not complete their learning.

I am going to leave it there for now.

After all that, I eventually came to in the living room and the hypnotherapist was white and panicking. Neither tape recorder had anything on it, even though they had both been running and the hypnotherapist had nothing on his pad except a few squiggles which neither of us could understand.

I have never ever forgotten what I experienced that day; it is etched on me for life. Often I question how, why and where I got all that, why the hypnotherapist was in such a state over some of the things he heard me say and why he didn't want any more to do with it.

This is a fascinating case and illustrates just how important it is to allow yourself to go beyond the light if you feel so compelled. It's not always necessary, but going to the death of the character you are reviewing, for me, is. If you don't, it's like reading a book and finding someone has ripped out the last page – you need to know what happened.

What was related in the afterlife part of this regression has been said before by many people, with the exception of God being an acronym. How fascinating – does that mean God is an organization? Can you imagine that, God being a corporation?! I think, though, that the idea is that God is whatever or whoever you want him, her or it to be. We have the most powerful and creative minds, if only we could recognize it. We are God and God is us. We work through him or her or it and he, she or it works through us. Names are irrelevant – it's how you feel about your god that matters.

How do you feel? Do you know? Try the following visualization, but be warned, it's very powerful and you may find it touches long-hidden emotions, so have some hankies at the ready.

Sit down somewhere comfortable, wearing loose clothing and ideally not just after you have eaten or when you're starving hungry. Light a candle if you wish, burn some incense (frankincense is a good one for this) and put on some beautiful music.

Imagine you're in your forest. See the forest, build it around you and really put yourself in it. Imagine the sights and sounds.

Now see a path ahead of you leading to a clearing, a well-tended space.

In that clearing you see a giant oak tree, a pulsating, shining tree. In its base there's a doorway. Move towards it.

Let the door open and walk through it into a room with a black-and-white floor. Take some time to look around you. If you've been here before, is there anything new in this space, anything you haven't noticed before?

Now move towards the back of the room where you see a simple altar with a single blue flame on it.

Ahead of you there are two pillars and behind those pillars are three doorways, one in the centre, one to the right and another to the left. Move towards the door in the centre.

As you stand in front of the door, Sandalphon, the great archangel of humanity, appears in front of you. His robe is russet, gold, olive, red and yellow, the colours of the fields and forests, and his eyes are the most incredible blue.

He smiles and asks what your purpose is. Tell him you wish to be closer to your own godhead, to be able to feel part of the great divine.

He moves towards the central door and, simply by drawing a magical symbol in the air, opens it for you.

You see a brilliant white light and Sandalphon asks you to step forward into it. Don't be afraid, you will be perfectly safe.

As you walk into the light and let it completely surround you, you start to feel calm, start to feel as if your cares and troubles are melting away, and you begin to smile as you haven't smiled in ages. You start to feel like a child, excited at what lies ahead but with no expectations.

As your eyes become accustomed to the light you see you're in a white cathedral, but it's like no cathedral you've ever seen before – it's inside and it's outside, it's on Earth and it's in space, it feels as if it encompasses everything but it still feels intimate.

Ahead of you there are some stairs, seven in fact, and at the top of those stairs there seem to be two giant hands. Move closer until you can see that, yes, that's exactly what they are!

Put yourself into these safe hands, let them hold you without restricting you and let them comfort you. Feel the healing from them and remember the peace and tranquillity they bring.

Now they start to move and seem to lift you up. As they do so you can hear music, angelic music that seems to grow in intensity the higher you go.

How high you go depends on how high you go!

There will be a point where you stop, a point where you are held there in the hands of ... who, what? Accept the healing, accept the love and accept the protection you receive and ask any questions you want. You may not get answers, but that's OK, you know that simply means not yet ... not yet.

Now you're being lowered to the top of those seven steps and placed very gently back onto the ground. As you walk away from those hands, say thank you for the privilege.

Walk now towards the light and into the room with the black-and-white tiled floor and into the waiting arms of Sandalphon. He will remind you that you're back on Earth and that you live your life as master of your own creation.

Thank him and walk out of the room and into the clearing.

As you walk away from the tree, see the door close.

Walk back to the path you started your journey from.

Walk through your forest and as you do so, let it fade away, let it melt away... Bring your consciousness back into the room you're in.

Kettle on, biscuits out and write your experience down as soon as you can!

How did you feel? What did you feel? What did you learn?

Do you now see some worries as being less important than they once were?

CHAPTER 11

MYTHICAL LIVES

What about mythical lives, the ones people tell you aren't real? What if you remember being in Atlantis or at King Arthur's court? Did those places really exist? I have seen regressions from many places that are considered mythical and the words 'No smoke without fire' come to mind.

It is worth noting that people who do not know each other and live in different countries report the same or similar things when they visit these lives. Here's one such story from Kirsty, from Brisbane, Australia:

In this life I have been single now for the last eight and a half years. My parents both came from the UK. My mum died on 28 December 1991 and her ashes are scattered out with the whales and dolphins just off the Queensland coast at Hervey Bay. My dad lives in

Redcliffe and my brother still lives with him. We aren't really close and my brother and I are like chalk and cheese. We are civil to each other, but that's about it really. I have one son whose name is Ben.

I used to be part of a spiritual family, a cult, but I took a big step and left. I returned all the crystals I had been given, including my chakra set, the gold ankh we all had to wear and a book I had borrowed.

Two days after I walked away I found an advert for a job with a company I had left eight and a half years before. I contacted them and got an interview and got the job on the spot! Coincidence maybe, but things obviously happen for a reason and if I hadn't left the cult I know I would not be the happy person I am at the moment. Things are definitely looking a lot better!

As for my past lives, I was about ten or twelve when one morning I heard on the radio about a young boy in England who had had a spider crawl up the inside of the sleeve of his school blazer and bite him on the eye. I went out and told Mum what I had just heard. She didn't know what I was talking about because she hadn't heard the broadcast. I listened to the news again and again and there was nothing more about it. I even watched the evening news and still there was nothing. Later I went through every newspaper we had in the house and I couldn't find the story, but I was sure I had seen it written down somewhere. I can still see the picture in my mind. Although it was in black and white, I know the uniform was a navy-blue blazer with a grey pinstripe and the school emblem on the pocket, a navy-blue hat a bit like the ones cricketers wear, a white buttoned shirt, dark grey knee-length shorts and grey knee-high socks and black shoes. The boy had a patch over his left eye and his parents were also in the picture with him. No one was smiling. At the time I put it all down to an early-morning dream, but now part of me feels that it was a past life, because it felt so familiar to me and how else would I know the colours of a uniform in a black-and-white picture?

I have since had regressions with a woman called Lea and in another past life I'm in a coffin, a very basic one, just a wooden box. It has collapsed onto my legs, obviously from the weight of all the dirt on top, and I'm being buried alive! I'm crying and screaming and scratching at the wood, wanting to get out and waiting for someone to find me and realize that I'm still alive, but all the time I know nobody will be coming and that I am going to die. The panic of not being able to breathe properly! I really don't like that one because the feeling of panic still gets to me!

I've also found myself in Atlantis, where my name is Mayahalina and I'm a priestess. Lea guided every thought and feeling and described what I should be seeing during that regression, so I don't know if the gorgeous blue water, the white sand, the crystal-encrusted caves, the emerald-green river and the waterfalls were real. Yet things also came to me without her help. At one point I was standing in front of my house in between two stone pillars looking out over the houses lower down the hillside to the water beyond. I could see my long hair gently moving in the breeze and feel it against my face. I was wearing a long dress, slightly off-white in colour, made of the softest, finest fabric. The top of the dress would be best described as Egyptian, with three rows of gold and moonstones around the neckline and shoulders. The third row from the top separated at the middle and went down the front of the dress to just above the waist and went around to the back to form a belt of sorts. I love to go back to that moment just to feel the calmness and serenity. I feel at peace then and I don't have a worry in the world.

I don't know if I can research anything about Mayahalina and Atlantis. As for the spider and the coffin, I wouldn't know where to start. But my past-life experiences have affected me in that I cannot stand spiders! Even if I just see one on television or in a book, I'm out of there. Also, I'm not really fond of small spaces and I'd already decided even before I found out about being buried alive that I would be cremated.

The past life in Atlantis – well, I would love to know for sure. I know Mayahalina fits somewhere. All my life, whenever I've been on the phone I've doodled 'M', and I thought it must have something to do with a past life somewhere.

I just want to say that I'm getting my life back on the path I want to be on now and not being pushed along someone else's path.

Don't be pushed along anyone's path, indeed! There's a lot in Kirsty's regression, phobias as well as mythical – sorry, *so-called* mythical – events to take in, and there's a lot to learn.

One thing Kirsty has to think about is just who does she tell about what's been going on? Should she tell anyone at all? Some may say she should, but consider the power of silence. Have you ever kept a secret? Something there's no need for anyone else to know about you? By keeping things to yourself you avoid ridicule or other people spoiling things, but the real deal in silence is conserving power and simply knowing where to go when you need to feel reassurance or strength. Kirsty says she often draws on her Atlantean life for calmness and serenity, which is a very good use of a past-life experience. Whenever you need comfort, strength or courage, just draw those memories to you.

CHAPTER 12

PHOBIAS

One of the things Kirsty believed came from a past-life experience was her phobia of spiders. Some people undertake past-life regression with the specific aim of finding out more about a phobia and possibly curing it. In my experience, phobias cannot be cured with one regression. It's an ongoing process – you identify where the phobia came from then deal with it using various techniques. This is best done with a therapist if you feel your phobia is getting in the way of living your life. But past-life regression can definitely help with locating the source of the problem.

Here's an unusual phobia that was identified through a past-life regression:

My name is Sharon and I'm from Gateshead. I'm a 37-year-old single woman, the daughter of a Geordie father and Glaswegian mother. I'm a teacher in a medium-secure adolescent psychiatric facility.

Ever since I can remember, I have always been absolutely terrified of nuns and priests. I can distinctly remember being at home at the age of three, being looked after by my father, when there was a knock at the door. I remember reaching up to open it and then becoming utterly hysterical upon seeing two nuns standing there. I can still recall the feeling of total fear.

My dad was totally baffled by my reaction and despite his reassurance that these women were 'good' people and that there was nothing to be afraid of, I was inconsolable. This feeling of terror has subsided slightly now that I'm an adult, but the hairs on the back of my neck still stand up whenever I see those long black robes.

I was very intrigued by my seemingly irrational fear of nuns. No one in my family could explain it. As I got older, however, images began to come into my head as though I were watching a slide show. The only way I can describe the images is to say they were like flashbacks.

I began picturing a field in the countryside with a primitive round wooden fence around another wooden structure. The wood was very dark in colour. I would then sense myself inside the wooden building, in a dark tower, trying desperately to get out but not being able to do so. I would see the image of flames and sense chaos all around me.

I knew that I had never been involved in a fire, nor had I ever been to the place I was visualizing. At the time I believed that I simply had a very vivid imagination.

At the age of 11, I developed a passion for France and all things French, despite never having been to France. No one in my family or social circle had ever shown any interest in the place or language and my parents were baffled by my Francophilia. I cannot explain it, but I felt an overwhelming need to be in France.

When I was 16, for my O-level History exam I had to do a project on Durham Cathedral. During a school visit there, I remember leaning against one of the pillars inside the cathedral and then screaming in fright when a priest suddenly appeared from the other side. I was very embarrassed about having made a scene in a quiet holy place of worship, but I still really struggled to mask my repulsion towards the priest, who was attempting to apologize for startling me. Needless to say, I was told off by one of my teachers for disturbing the silence.

At the risk of sounding conceited, I excelled at the French language and went on to complete a degree in French Studies at Lancaster University. In 1991, as part of my degree course, I went to live in Châtillon-sur-Seine, near Dijon, in the Burgundy region of France. I can remember being so excited about finally achieving my ambition of living in France. Not long into my year abroad, however, I began to experience flashbacks of people in black robes standing in a circle and chanting in the darkness. Although I couldn't actually see myself, I knew I was there and I really didn't like it. I could sense evil in the chanting and I had the feeling that I was there against my will.

Very quickly after my arrival in France, I became desperately unhappy for no apparent reason. I constantly felt suffocated and on edge. Rationally, I fully accepted that this could be attributed to depression brought on by numerous factors, but I just knew something awful was going to happen to me if I stayed. I felt imprisoned.

One weekend I was driving through the Champagne region when I saw a sign that said 'Champignon'. Although I had never been there, I was totally convinced that I had visited the place before. I'm still not sure if my friend and travelling companion believed me. She probably still thinks I'm crazy!

It was not until much later, 1996 in fact, when I was having some faith healing that I was told by the healer that she and I had been novice nuns in a convent in Champignon that had been burnt to the ground because black magic had been practised there. Apparently, the mother superior of the convent had been chasing us for centuries for our refusal to participate in the 'dark arts' and had told the healer that she would never let the 'young one' – me – go!

I would have been extremely sceptical if I had not sat in a development circle about a month prior to this and had the spirit of a very serene, beautiful nun appear to me. Then her face suddenly contorted into the most horrific thing I have ever seen, with fangs coming towards me, hissing at me. I really thought I was going to die of fear that night. My heart felt as though it was going to burst, but I had been told not to break the circle, so I sat still and silently begged for someone to help me. Then my guides came and helped me out.

If you are wondering how the faith healer knew about the convent, she'd been regressed and had gone back to her past life there. I still have difficulty in processing such a bizarre chain of events...

I didn't experience any more paranormal experiences until March this year, 2008, when I was in Austria visiting a former convent in Herzogenburg. As I was walking through the courtyard I suddenly heard monks chanting very loudly. I asked my Austrian friends if this was a gimmick to create a 'holy' atmosphere, but they looked very puzzled and told me that they hadn't heard anything and that there were no monks in the building. I was astonished – the chanting had been very loud and very creepy, I thought. I heard it reverberating around the square again as we were leaving, but my friends insisted that they couldn't hear anything.

Although I do believe in Spiritualism, past lives, etc., I often question whether it can all be explained by psychology or imagination. I am also still somewhat nervous in case there is the malevolent spirit of a nun waiting to harm me!

Wow! What an experience. Sharon felt the influence from her past life early in her current incarnation and it followed through so strongly she was drawn to a place she may have inhabited in a former existence. Her doubts about past lives may be put to rest if she has a regression with a qualified and recommended therapist, and her fears over the nun she sees as such a horrific character could be allayed by doing what we all know we need to do when we have a fear: face it, in the knowledge that help will come from many places – your guides, your soul mates incarnate, but mostly from your own soul and your ability to remember and to use the gifts you have to overcome adversity. Those who have harmed us, no matter what their guise and costume, can have an effect on us from incarnation to incarnation, but we can face up to that and overcome it.

It seems as if Sharon is continuing to get little proofs, little nudges to do something more about this time she had in France, and that may be because this life is a key life, a life that has a very strong influence on her current incarnation. If re-solved, imagine the peace it could bring.

Sharon may already be on her way to achieving that. She is clearly on a spiritual path, one that's being driven by her soul, and, as I know, when the soul speaks, the personality will step aside!

CHAPTER 13

NEW WAYS TO FIND YOUR OLD WAYS

If you really want to find out more about your past lives, there are many ways of doing it. We have already established that you can dream about them, receive clues about them in your daily life and revisit them in regression with a hypnotherapist, a regression therapist, a psychic or on your own. You can even do it in a workshop situation, as Amanda from Hastings relates:

I attended your past-lives workshop in London last week. I thoroughly enjoyed it.

During my visit to the Akashic records I needed to release my habit of not finishing things, so you asked me to email you my experience by midday on Saturday. Well, I hope this reaches you in time – as you can see, I've left it to the last moment!

My animal companion during this meditation was a black jaguar, which was wonderful, as I adore cats of all kinds. I found myself stroking and caressing his thick fur, which gave me comfort as I was feeling nervous. [Jaguars are very powerful animal guides. They symbolize authority and are associated with South American shamanism in particular.]

On the walls of the great building I saw the Tower tarot card. I have had this card occur on several occasions over the past five years. Unfortunately, during that time I have had a major bereavement and a huge amount of upheaval in my family life, including my nephew with special needs coming to live with us, which has caused severe stress, particularly to my youngest son, who developed an unusual illness which led to a year off school. Hence, the Tower was not a card I wanted to see again. [Fortunately, it can also mean an end to such upheaval when used in a healing context such as past-life regression.]

On the door of the building were two symbols. On the right door, which was studded and wooden, was the infinity sign; on the plain wooden left door was an open triangle.

I did not notice anything in particular in the corridor.

In the reading room of the Akashic records, I do not remember the book in detail, apart from noting it was old brown leather (battered like me!) and quite thick. But it felt warm and smelt comforting. When I opened it, things happened quickly:

1. *I saw a field of wheat and realized this was from a past life I had worked on before. I was a young woman in my late teens and a miller's daughter. I was raped by a man I recognized as the neighbour I was having problems with in my current life – in fact, I was doing the past-life regression to find out why I was having so many problems with him. In the past life I got pregnant and died in childbirth. Thankfully, I have been able to work with my angels and guides and release the fear and resentment from that time. That, along with a sturdy fence, has led to a big improvement in my relationship with my neighbour.*

2. *I was a Japanese sailor, I think during the First World War, although that might not be so. The boat sank. At first I thought I'd drowned but then realized*

I'd survived. I hope to go back and work on this, as I love being near water but have a problem being over it. Actually, I have more of a problem with bridges than boats. Odd.

3. *I was in a medieval walled settlement. I was some kind of servant. There was straw on the floor and the smells and sounds of horses. I was a man, but I felt more like a woman, so perhaps I was gay. I was waiting on my master. I was quite happy.*

I left behind my inability to finish things or not see them through to the end and asked for the ability to follow things through to their conclusion. I also asked for abundance and happiness, as I have been rather depressed recently.

During the workshop I met a new guide, a woman called Lucielle or Lucy. She's very tall and I think she's going to nag me about my health. The night afterwards I heard a woman's voice. It wasn't a familiar voice. I felt panicky and asked her not to talk to me again, but to tell me who she was. Then the words just 'happened' in my head, like a thought, which is my usual experience of communication with guides. She said, 'Lucielle,' but I think she was a bit irritated with me!

Then last night I heard a man's voice. Again I was chicken and asked him not to talk again. I think it was my guide Ronin, a rather cool Frenchman. I'm going to be brave and ask him to talk to me again. But not in bed in the dark – why do they do that? [Because your mind is calmer then and they can!]

Amanda shows just how much can be achieved in one day's workshop. By attending, she gained the tools to access her own past lives and to think about how they affected this current incarnation and how she could use them to release negativity and work with guides. This is heartwarming for me – the more people know what they are truly capable of, the easier things can be, and what better than to see that in others?!

Well done, Amanda, you're an inspiration!

But what about spontaneous past-life regression? One minute there you are, walking down the street, then wham! Past life?

Jeff from Toronto wrote to me about his experience:

I don't know what this was – a dream, a lucid dream, a past-life regression? I don't have the faintest idea, but here it is.

About 20 years ago I was lying in bed. I wasn't awake, but I wasn't asleep either. According to my girlfriend I started talking nonsense and I remember my surroundings changed, just melted away, and I saw myself in the old French fort of Louisburg, on Cape Breton Island in Nova Scotia, Canada. I'd never been there in my life, but it was if I was walking through the streets of the town/fortress in the 1750s. According to my girlfriend, I was talking about how the soldiers (whom I saw dressed mostly in white-and-blue uniforms) got angry with us children (I think I was about ten in this vision) when we played up on the battlements. They kept yelling that we were going to hurt ourselves and to get down now. I remembered tethered goats as well.

And that was it – I snapped back into the present and found a very puzzled girlfriend looking at me with a very worried expression!

Sometime later I found a book on Louisburg and had a look through it. The fort was built by Louis XVI and captured in 1758 or thereabouts largely by James Wolfe, who captured Quebec not too long afterwards. It was torn down by the Brits but the Canadian government rebuilt it in the 1970s and early 80s. A lot of the streets and buildings were very familiar to me and one or two things clanged as being 'inaccurate' and not as I remembered them.

It may well be nothing, but there was such a sense of reality about it all when it was happening. I've never been to Louisburg, by the way.

That's the only time that's happened with me, but I have had other strange experiences. One night I was being brought home by a date when all of a sudden it was daytime. The freeway was gone and I was on, of all things, a wagon like in the old west. I could see the horses in front of me, smell and feel the dust from the plains and hear the sounds around me. I was holding a baby in my arms. I have never been blessed with having a baby and I remember the contented feeling I had with this child. I could see the plains around me and feel the quiet solitude of the country. Then just as quickly, it was night again and I was back on the freeway.

The same thing has happened to me twice when I have visited the Alamo in San Antonio,

*Texas. When you walk into the main build-
ing there is a man or woman holding a sign
to ask you to please be respectful as this is a
shrine. The place is always filled with visitors,
but the first time I went I saw none of the visitors but instead saw men in period clothing
with rifles. The place was noisy, with people
talking. There was a window on the wall facing the front door. It was very high up and
I saw two men pacing back and forth along
the wall. There was a ledge there; I remember my eyes going to the ladders which were
propped against it. The two men both had rifles; one had his resting against his shoulder
while the other was holding his in his right
hand. Both looked out of the window when
they passed it. Then the noise went away, the
vision faded and I was back in the shrine. I
saw the multitude of people again and looked
back at the ledge. The two men were gone. I
will never forget that as long as I live.*

Jeff never had a regression but his mind took him
back to another time, and what's interesting is that
it seems to have happened when he was awake
as well as when he was asleep. Scientists will tell
you the mid-point between waking and sleeping is
when the subconscious mind creates random im-

186

ages. They may have a point, though let's not fall into the trap of assuming science is always right. Perhaps Jeff was actually in a state where his soul could communicate with much more clarity and his personality actually got the message.

Regardless of what state of awareness he was in, these were both powerful experiences. It's the sense of reality he mentions that's important. Knowing the difference between what seems like a daydream and what falls harder on your memory is crucial, and knowing your own truth more so.

What Jeff should do next is the question. Clearly a past-life regression could help and by the sounds of things Jeff would be likely to get details that would give him his personal proofs. Hopefully one day he will want to!

Why Not Google?

Talking of getting proof of past lives, some of the greatest evidence comes from our modern obsession with the Internet. A search engine can save years of investigation, as Cassandra found out...

My name is Cassandra and I live in Kent with my partner Greg and our Old English Sheepdog Rufus. We have no children. I spend my time walking the dog and doing spiritual development, either meditating, doing tarot and psychic readings or paranormal investigations. I am working towards a full-time job putting my clairvoyant skills to good use, hopefully on investigations, but who knows what else might come up!

I was doing the Akashic records meditation. This time my usual forest guide, a deer, turned into a brown horse.

Arriving at the library, I found my entrance door was yellow with symbols that looked a cross between cave paintings and hieroglyphics. Upon entering the corridor, I could see artefacts on either side: first a long spear, then a cloth with the same symbols as the door. I also saw a clay pot and some animal skins hanging on the walls.

The next door was opened by a large man who looked like a Native American. He wore animal furs. He showed me to my book and I saw the cover was also made of animal fur; it was brown and soft like velvet. There were two words embroidered in gold-coloured thread on the front which I understood to be my name. The first was very clear, the second I could not make out.

Opening the book, I saw a moving picture on the page of me as a Native American holding a spear. I was approaching a hilltop followed by other tribesmen. Seeing our prey was close and cornered, we spread out and ran down the hill to attack. This was the moment when the picture became bigger and bigger until I was a part of the scene. Throwing our spears, we caught our prey, which looked to me like a buffalo.

Suddenly the scene changed and we were sitting in a circle around a large fire eating our feast. A drink was passed around which seemed like some sort of alcohol. After the meal, each of us chewed on a stick which tasted hot but refreshing at the same time, kind of like cinnamon. There was dancing and chanting and singing. I felt a strong association with spirituality and bears – we seemed to praise bears.

I felt it was time to leave, so I closed the book and my guide came to escort me out. I recognized him as one of the tribe. The artefacts on the way out were more detailed; there were bear skins and headdresses as well as footwear.

An Internet search showed the name I had

was part of a Native American tribe's name. The tribe has been going for thousands of years and still exists today. Although I found no evidence of the person I had been, at least that word is in use, so I consider that to be a good positive sign.

I have not revisited that life since. However, a few weeks before this particular regression I had asked to meet my doorkeeper during a separate meditation and had had a very clear image of a Native American with a bearskin on. [A doorkeeper is a special guide, one who protects your mind as you go through life. Doorkeepers are often seen as fierce individuals – people you wouldn't mess with! They are there to put the old saying 'You only get what you can handle' into action.] *The head of the bear was worn as a headdress, something I had never seen or heard of before. In fact, I had never been particularly interested in 'all that Native American stuff'. I knew they were supposed to be spiritual people but that's all, so this was an extra surprise and has prompted me to find out more.*

I did an Internet search which revealed on that exact day, 22 December, the winter sol-

stice, there was a Native American celebration for the hibernation of the bear. This is a ritual which involves dancing, something I love. While this dance takes place, the ghost of the bear comes to cleanse the area and then a fire is lit. There is dancing and chanting and the spirits of the ancestors of the tribe join in the dance. Eventually the bear is lulled to sleep for the winter. See www.calicoghostwalk.com/BearDance1.htm.   I could not believe my eyes when I found this article, particularly as it was the exact day I had asked to meet my doorkeeper! Since then I have met him in meditation and he sometimes takes the form of a large bear, but usually appears on a brown horse and with his headdress on. The second time I saw him I asked what I should call him and he replied, 'You know me as Big Bear.'

Could my past life have been showing me involved in the bear ritual? Is this why my doorkeeper shows himself as a bear sometimes?

The past-life experience, along with meeting my doorkeeper, has prompted me to look into Native American culture, which, as I said, I had no idea about or interest in before my experiences. I feel a closer connection with my doorkeeper now and feel I almost know him. I wonder if I did know him in that life. Is that possible? I realize now that I can learn a lot from other cultures and hope to revisit that particular life to find out more.

This life is interesting because of the spiritual content in it, especially given Cassie's interest in the subject in this incarnation. Her symbolism is also intriguing, as the deer changes into a horse; the deer symbolizes love, gentleness, kindness, gracefulness, sensitivity, purity of purpose, walking in the light, and is swift, meek and gentle, whereas the horse is all about stamina, mobility, strength and power, coping under difficult circumstances, love, devotion, loyalty, the land and travel. One is more passive than the other, although both are strong animals. For me this shift is about Cassie taking control of her path. She says in her letter that she wants to pursue her gifts, which is of course a conscious decision to move from the safety of her forest into the wide open plains and the adventures they bring.

Symbolism is very important in your own regressions and taking note of any animals or other guides that come your way is crucial. If you don't have a symbol dictionary, there's your old friend the Internet – so useful!

Cassie also experienced a shift in her awareness of all things Native American. That is a strong and very beautiful culture that holds many awakenings for those who are prepared to go beyond the obvious lures of feathers and turquoise jewellery! The fact that Cassie's new-found interest comes from a past life will make her learning so much easier for her and I have no doubt it will supply her with many a revelation.

As for whether she could have known her doorkeeper in another life, as with all guides, the answer is 'yes'. You are likely to see guides in your past-life regressions, so use this experience to ask them questions and to interact with them. All information is valid – have I said that before? If I have, it must be important!

Who Becomes a Past-Life Therapist?

When you have had a few regressions of your own it's only natural to want others to feel the benefit. Most people encourage their mates to go along to a therapist, but some take it a step further and become therapists themselves. I am not from the school that says there are some people who are gifted in this area and some who aren't. We all have the potential; then it's a question of training and enthusiasm.

Jeff Powell is one of those people who has taken his interest that bit further. He wrote to me asking to use some of my visualizations as part of his own studies to become a past-life regression therapist. I am pleased to say his results have been superb and he clearly has a great understanding of the process involved and a gentleness in the way he executes a past-life regression. I have included several of Jeff's regressions here to show that becoming a past-life regression therapist is within the grasp of us all, given good training and of course the willingness to put the effort in!

Jeff himself explains:

I am a paranormal investigator, a Spiritualist medium and Reiki practitioner and am just about to do my final exams to be a past-life regression therapist.

This was the first of my past-life regressions. It was done on my partner, Carolyn Green. I was delighted with the results.

Carolyn

I am a divorced mother of four children. I went through 15 years of domestic violence from my husband and am currently in the final year of a degree in health and social care. I am a Spiritualist medium, paranormal investigator and qualified nail technician.

JP: Can you tell me what year it is?

CG: It is 1882.

JP: Look down at your feet and describe what you are wearing.

CG: I am wearing short black boots. They look a little scruffy.

JP: Work your way up your body and describe what you are wearing.

CG: I am wearing maid's clothing, brown and white. There are lots of layers and a white frilly cap.

JP: Look at your feet once more and describe what you are standing on.

CG: I am standing on stone flooring. It's light yellow in colour, like Yorkshire stone.

JP: Tell me about the landscape you can see in front of you.

CG: I am in the grounds of a large mansion. The perimeter is framed by very tall trees. There are beautifully lawned gardens all around the building.

JP: Can you describe the house for me?

CG: It is an old Georgian house with huge windows and doors throughout. There are ten bedrooms in total, with servants' quarters at the rear of the house.

JP: What is your name?

CG: My name is Eliza. I don't know my proper surname. I am an orphan.

JP: How old are you?

CG: I am 21 years old.

JP: What country are you in here?

CG: I am in England.

JP: What part of this country?

CG: I am in Southwark, Surrey. I have just travelled from Nottingham.

JP: Turn around and look and tell me if you see anyone.

CG: There is a woman who is in charge of all the maids. She is my new boss. She is dressed in black clothes and a black cap. Her name is Ann. I have not been here long and she has taken me under her wing.

JP: How do you feel at this moment?

CG: I feel happy, relaxed and not afraid any more. This family has saved me... I felt a bit panicky at first and didn't know what to expect. I had been treated badly by my former owner and had chains on my ankle. I am happy this family treats me like a human being. They are kind to me.

JP: There is a mirror near to you. Can you look at it and tell me what you see?

CG: I am small in height and very slightly built. I have long brown curly hair and blue eyes. I have red marks above my boots from the chains and shackles.

JP: Tell me what you find yourself doing here today. What is your purpose?

CG: I have been given a job and been taken in by the house. I clean in the morning and look after the children in the afternoon.

JP: Can you tell me more about the family?

CG: They are a nice family. The head of the house is Paul ... Paul Sommerfield. His wife is away visiting her sick mother, so I have not met her yet. The children are adorable. They are Tom, who is 12 years old, Sue, who is seven and with whom I have formed an instant bond – I cannot describe it but it is as if I have known her all her life – and last of all, there's young Harry, who is just five years old.

(Carolyn was reluctant to go back in time in this lifetime, so I took her forward to a significant event.)

JP: Where do you find yourself now?

CG: I am in the same house as previously. I have just had a baby.

JP: How far forward in time have you gone?

CG: It is 1896 and I am now 35 years of age.

JP: Can you tell me more about your life at this time?

CG: I have just given birth to a beautiful baby girl whom we have named Elizabeth. I also have a lovely boy of five years of age called Ralph. I am married to Matthew and we live in a small cottage in the grounds.

JP: Can you describe and tell me more about your husband, Matthew, and how you met?

CG: Matthew is around 5 ft 8 inches. He is slim, with a moustache and dark hair. He wears smart working clothes – black boots, three-quarter length tartan trousers, a white shirt and brown waistcoat. He is 36 years old.

His name is Matthew Waterfield. He moved from Northamptonshire and joined the house to work in the stables. I was a little shy around him at first but there was an instant connection with him. We married two years after meeting. He is kind and treats me well. We are very happy together and he is a good father. He is a hard grafter and always thinks of his family before himself.

(At this point I take Carolyn forward to another significant event in her life.)

JP: Where do you find yourself now?

CG: It is a couple of months later. It is Lizzy's christening. The house has given us all the day off and thrown a party for us. They are so good to us. Most of the people from the village are here. It is one of the happiest times of our lives. We are dancing around; it's like barn dancing. We have lots of friends now and lots of gifts from everybody. Lots of beer and wine are had by all.

(At this point I take Carolyn forward to another significant event in her life.)

JP: Where do you find yourself now?

CG: It's 1902. I am in bed, very ill. I have not eaten in ages and feel weak. We are still living in the cottage. My lungs are bad; I have consumption. It's not getting better. I think I am dying. I have not been ill for very long ... about two weeks.

Matthew and my 11-year-old son Ralph are at my bedside now. I feel all floaty and now I am looking at myself in bed with people crying around me. I see somebody reaching out to me. I get the feeling it is my mother and reach out to her.

JP: Do you feel you know anybody from that lifetime in your present life? Remember, looking into their eyes can tell you this. They say the eyes are the windows to your eternal soul.

CG: Yes. I knew I had a connection with Sue, who was one of the children I looked after. She is my sister Gill in this lifetime. We are very close.

I brought Carolyn back from her regression. We researched it a little and came up with:

- Elizabeth Waterfield, born around 1863 in Nottinghamshire
- Elizabeth Waterfield, born around 1894 in Surrey
- Matthew Waterfield, born around 1864 in Northamptonshire
- Ralph Waterfield, born around 1889 in Leicestershire

- Louisa Elizabeth Waterfield, born 1896 in Southwark, Surrey.

These are all close matches but not confirmed or linked as yet. Research is ongoing.

Carolyn says:

I felt uneasy about going back from 1882 to see my earlier life as a slave, but I was excited about what I experienced through the regression. It felt as though I was looking down on a scene from a drama. It was also very emotional for me. The experience left me feeling drained and spaced-out for a day or two.

It has got me thinking more about other past lives I have been through and I am eager to do some more regressions.

The feeling of being drained is a common one. It usually passes very quickly, but remember to eat and drink after a regression, even if it's just a biscuit and a cup of tea!

Carolyn mentions how emotional the experience was for her. Emotion is the key to a full regression. It brings the truth of it home and offers the chance to release energy we may have been carrying for centuries.

For a first regression both Jeff and Carolyn did a great job and no wonder Carolyn wants to do more, but remember to give yourself time not only to research the life you have discovered but also to learn from the interpersonal relationships you have found and from the most important relationship – the one with yourself.

That life seemed to be showing Carolyn that even after a rough start a happy ending can happen, which echoes her life now. Although her ex didn't make an appearance, perhaps it's too soon to see what life that has come from, if indeed it has come from a past life...

Now for Jeff, who was regressed by a friend, AH:

Jeff

I live in the Wirral, England, at the moment, with my girlfriend Carolyn. I have three children from my previous marriage. I am a Spiritualist medium, past-life regression therapist, Reiki practitioner, paranormal investigator with *Most Haunted* Ghost Tours and PC technician.

AH: Can you tell me what year it is?

JP: It is 1872.

AH: Look down at your feet and describe what you are wearing.

JP: I am wearing black shoes. They look shiny and new.

AH: Work your way up your body and describe what you are wearing.

JP: I am wearing a navy-blue dress and a white pinafore with a tight-fitting corset underneath which feels very uncomfortable. But appearances are everything.

AH: Look at your feet once more and describe what you are standing on.

JP: I am standing on a highly polished wooden floor.

AH: Can you describe the house for me?

JP: It is a very large Georgian mansion with eight huge bedrooms. It has five bathrooms and some secret corridors. It is built on four acres of beautiful countryside and is surrounded by glorious gardens.

AH: What is your name?

JP: My name is Elizabeth, Elizabeth Ida Davidson, but I am known as Ida.

AH: How old are you?

JP: I am 27 years of age.

AH: What country are you in here?

JP: I am in England.

AH: What part of this country?

JP: I am in Kentish Town.

AH: Turn around and look and tell me if you see anyone.

JP: Near to me is my butler, Samuel.

AH: Can you describe him for me?

JP: He has been good, loyal and trustworthy in the five years he has been with us. He is stout in build, smartly dressed, as always. He is wearing a white shirt, black trousers, three-quarter length jacket and highly polished shoes. He is an asset to the house.

AH: There is a mirror near to you on the wall. Can you look at it and tell me what you see?

JP: I am very elegant with black hair put up at the back. I am average in height and build. I have smooth soft silky skin. I am very proud of my appearance and believe it's important to always look one's best.

AH: Tell me what you find yourself doing here today. What is your purpose?

JP: I am the lady of the house and I oversee everything whilst my husband is out. I am stoking the fire now; it is a grand fireplace which produces a great amount of heat.

My butler Samuel comes into the room and announces, 'George Davidson here to see you, ma'am.'

My brother-in-law has just arrived. He and my husband Henry have been out all morning hunting for deer. My husband is taking the deer to the kitchen at the rear of the house.

AH: Can you describe your brother-in-law and husband for me and tell me how you met?

JP: George is 22 years of age, well dressed and the younger brother of my Henry. He is single but is never without a girl on his arm. He is a bit of a ladies' man, whereas my husband is the opposite: he is quiet, mild-mannered and well respected in our community. He is tall, handsome and was the only man for me as soon as I looked into his eyes in the dance hall at my cousin's wedding. He is a few years older than I and I am very proud of him, as he is of me. We are a match made in heaven. It is coming up to our tenth anniversary soon. He is always well dressed. Even when he is out hunting he looks dapper.

(At this point I am taken forward to a significant event in that lifetime.)

AH: Where do you find yourself now?

JP: I have just given birth to our first child, a son we have named Daniel.

AH: How far forward in time have you gone?

JP: It is 1879. I am now 34 years of age.

AH: Can you tell me what you find yourself doing here today and what is significant to this part of your lifetime?

JP: I am holding my son Daniel. I feel so proud. We have wanted a child for so many years and we have both longed for this moment. I have my family around the bed – Henry, my mother and my younger brother Elliot. They take turns holding the baby. Henry is so proud of him. Now he has a son to carry on his name.

There is a midwife figure moving everyone out of the room. She is explaining to me how to breastfeed.

AH: Can you describe and tell me more about your brother and mother?

JP: My brother Elliot is now 31. He is the joker in the family. Whenever anyone is feeling down he will have them smiling in a jiffy. We are a close family and always have been very supportive of one another.

My mother's name is Charlotte. She is now 73 years of age. We are very close and never have a bad word to say about each other. We have a special bond which I suppose all mothers and daughters should have. She gave me such a wonderful childhood, one that I will never forget.

(At this point I am taken forward to another significant event in that lifetime.)

AH: Where do you find yourself now?

JP: I am in the garden with my mother.

AH: How far forward in time have you gone?

JP: It is now 1899. It is July, 20 years later.

AH: Can you tell me what you find yourself doing here today and what is significant to this part of your lifetime?

JP: I am having drinks in the garden with my mother. We have white cast-iron table and chairs with a parasol. My mother has a gown over her head protecting her from the heat of the sun. We are talking about the children in our family.

(I start to cry at this moment.)

AH: Why are you upset at this moment in time?

JP: I have just realized that this is the last time I see my mother alive. She is so happy and has had a wonderful life. I am feeling the pain of losing her. She meant everything to me and she was my best friend as well as my mother. She died in her sleep that night.

AH: Do you feel you know anybody from that lifetime in your present life? Remember, looking into their eyes can tell you this. They say the eyes are the windows to your eternal soul.

JP: Yes, my mother in that lifetime was my nan in my lifetime now.

(I start to cry again and am brought back from my regression.)

From the information gathered in the regression:

- Elizabeth Ida Davidson, 1845–?
- Henry Davidson, 1843–?
- George Davidson, 1850–?
- Daniel Davidson, 1879–?
- Charlotte (do not know surname), 1806–99
- Elliot (do not know surname), 1848–?

After a little research on the Internet, the nearest matches to these on census records were:

- Elizabeth Davidson, born about 1843 in Devon, spouse Henry, resident in London 1891

- Henry Davidson, born about 1843 in Devon, spouse Elizabeth, resident in London 1891

- George Davidson, born about 1850 in Finsbury, Middlesex, resident in St Luke's, London, 1881

- Daniel Davidson, born about 1876, Woolwich, Kent, resident in London in 1901.

We have not yet found if this George and Daniel Davidson are linked to Elizabeth and Henry.

It took me a while to get used to being a woman in that life. I felt very upper class and proud of it. I also felt quite weird after the regression when I looked back on giving birth and breastfeeding.

As for the connection to my nan in this life, I can understand that. She passed away when I was 15 years old, but she was like a second mother to me and I spent a lot of my childhood sleeping at her house. She was a medium and read tea leaves. She told me I was special and had lovely healing hands. She was right – I am now a Spiritualist medium and a Reiki healer – but at the time I thought they were words nans usually said to their grandsons.

Jeff found it a little strange to experience a life as a woman, but if we can be of any creed and colour, then surely we can be of either sex and sometimes even in between! It's interesting that in the regression his language seems very feminine, and his point about how important it is to look good all the time made me chuckle!

It can certainly be fascinating the first time you change sex – you actually feel very girly or manly. And it's an interesting thought that just as our physical bodies can be either sex, so too can our souls. Maybe that explains a lot!

Think about that for a minute – do you have a male soul or a female one? And what does that entail? This isn't about being a man trapped in a female body or vice versa, it's about the essence of your soul being strongly male or strongly female. If you're a man with a female soul, you may empathize with others and be able to understand things well on an emotional level; if you're female with a male soul, you may be more driven to be in charge. These are of course generalizations; my job here is to promote debate, to give you more to think about and to leave you with more questions than answers. Annoying, isn't it?

Finally, here is a regression Jeff performed on Irene, a friend of his:

Irene

I am divorced and have lived on my own for over 20 years. I have three sons, six grandchildren and four great-grandchildren.

JP: Can you tell me what year it is?

IO: It is 1824.

JP: Look down at your feet and describe what you are wearing.

IO: I am wearing nothing on my feet.

JP: Work your way up your body and describe what you are wearing.

IO: I am wearing a blue top with blue shorts.

JP: Look at your feet once more and describe what you are standing on.

IO: I am standing on sand.

JP: Tell me about the landscape you can see in front of you.

IO: I am on a beach. The sea is in front of me. I see chalk and sandy rocks to the right of me. The sea is a beautiful shade of blue; the waves are flowing at my feet. Our house is behind me.

JP: Can you describe your house for me?

IO: It is a big white house with pillars on the front of it. It has beautiful gardens with gorgeous flowers and a swimming pool.

JP: What is your name?

IO: My name is Bertha ... Bertha Coppleton.

JP: How old are you?

IO: I am 22 years old

JP: What country are you in here?

IO: I am in Portugal.

JP: What part of this country?

IO: We live near Lisbon.

JP: Are you Portuguese?

IO: No, I am English.

JP: Can you tell me where you have lived previously?

IO: I was born in Redburn in the Highlands, Scotland. We moved to Essex when I was six years old. My father is an architect and built this house and now we live here.

JP: Turn around and look and tell me if you see anyone.

IO: I am with my father now in our garden. We are looking at people along the shoreline and I have been sunbathing.

JP: Can you tell me your father's name and tell me more about him?

IO: My father's name is Edward. He is 58 years old and is a very funny man. He makes us laugh so much. He has a mop of black hair, a moustache and a short beard. He is of average height and today he is wearing a white suit with a red scarf with spots. He is now smiling at me whilst smoking his pipe. He is an architect; he drew up the plans for this house and is very clever. He paints in his spare time and is a good artist.

JP: Can you now walk into your house and go to the nearest mirror? Can you look at it and tell me what you see?

IO: I am of average height and slim, but not too slim – just right. I have blue eyes and short dark hair. Father doesn't like my hair short, but I wanted a change from it being long.

JP: Now that you are inside the house, can you describe it for me?

IO: We have five bedrooms, of which mine is the biggest, a grand staircase turning to the right, three reception rooms and a big kitchen. We have gorgeous curtains which were sent from abroad by Father.

JP: Can you tell me more about your family?

IO: I am the only child. I work in a shop down the road called Popperton's. They make tea-cakes. My mother's name is Polly. She is 59 years of age and is a seamstress and makes beautiful dresses. She is tall and slim with copper-coloured hair which is going slightly grey in places. I have wonderful parents.

JP: What do you find yourself doing today?

IO: My best friend Betty Carlton has come around to see me. She is younger than me, 18, and she has lovely brown hair which she has tied up at the moment, with ribbons in. Her hair looks lovely when it is down, it is so long. She is very pretty. I have nicknamed her Betsy and she calls me Berty. Our families moved to Portugal together. I have known her for years.

(I take Irene forward to a significant event in that lifetime.)

JP: Where do you find yourself now?

IO: I am in the Red Cross Hospital, Lisbon.

JP: How far forward in time have you gone?

IO: It is 1846 and I am now 44 years of age.

JP: Can you tell me more about your life at this time?

IO: I am walking around checking all the nurses, making sure they are all right. I am a matron here. I live quite near to the hospital; in fact, it is on top of the hill and is called Whiteacres House. I am married now and have a son.

JP: Can you describe and tell me more about your husband and your son?

IO: My husband's name is David, David Dartford. He is English and we met in England and have a place in Highgate, London, as well as here in Lisbon. He is handsome with dark hair and bushy eyebrows.

Our son is called Brian. He is six years old now. He is always grubby. He is a bit too skinny, but a lovely lad.

It feels cold in this ward because the doors are open all the time.

(At this point I take Irene forward to another significant event in her life.)

JP: Where do you find yourself now?

IO: We are in London. It's 1874. Brian has taken me to Harley Street so I can see a doctor. I have got lots of things wrong with me now. I have something we would nowadays call Alzheimer's disease and my eyes are bad.

Mother and Father have passed away and left us their house by the sea in Lisbon.

We have to go shopping to get my husband Edward some things. He is in hospital and very ill. TB has set in and David is in a bad way. He has gone grey now but still looks handsome. It is cold now and we are going to our place in Highgate, but I just want to go home to Lisbon.

(At this point Irene starts to get upset. She is also confused, as her husband is David and not Edward. She is getting mixed up, maybe talking about her parents. I take her forward to another significant event in that life.)

JP: Where do you find yourself now?

IO: I am back in London. It is 1875. David has died. I am with Brian, my son. It's only days since the funeral. Brian lives in a flat by Harley Street and is a lawyer now. I can't cope without him. I am cold and want to go home now.

(At this point Irene gets upset again and I take her forward to the next significant event in her life.)

JP: Where do you find yourself now?

IO: I am at home in Lisbon. It is 1876. Brian has wheeled me out into the garden to my seat. I am going soon, I am dying. It's old age. And my eyes... I cannot see properly. I feel weak now, too weak to walk. I am dying... I am watching myself now. I have passed away...

(Irene now goes quiet and then gets upset. I bring her back from her regression.)

From the facts found during this regression, I have come up with:

- Bertha Coppleton/Dartford, 1802–1876
- Edward Coppleton, 1766–?
- Polly Coppleton, 1765–?
- Betty Carlton, 1806–?
- David Dartford, 1806–1875
- Brian Dartford, 1840–?

and have found:

- Elizabeth Carlton, born 1806, Westmorland, England, resident in Cumberland, 1871
- Lots of matches for Copperfield but no matching years for Coppleton.

Irene also felt spaced-out, she says, for a couple of days, which is a long time, but I suspect she went very deep. This shows the need to give yourself some space after your regression – don't expect to have it and then be frying chips that evening!

Jeff's work shows that it's possible to get a lot of information from the off and that's certainly true – your first regression is as valid as your twentieth one.

Irene's visuals were excellent, as was her recollection of facts, but remember not everyone will see their past lives that way. Sometimes you will see very little, but don't be downhearted – what you feel, what you sense, what you hear, what you just know is there is just as valid as lots of visual detail.

Always – no, make that *always* – write down what you get and go with anything else that comes to you in that process. Ultimately, of course, it's not how much information you get but what you do with it that matters. It's what you learn about yourself and what that knowledge brings to your life now.

Sometimes, as we have seen, you get two lives in one. Now, when the soul decides to show you more than one at a time, is that because it's in a hurry or just making a point?

As you uncover your past lives, you will come to understand what your soul is trying to tell you. You will see a pattern. Sometimes it can be tough to spot and at other times it can be blatantly obvious, but either way it will be there. It might be about things you could develop or things you should avoid or something else entirely – that's up to you to work out!

Here's a regression I performed that was about reasons why we sometimes do what we do and why we are so good at it...

Jennie

Jennie is a bright, bubbly, 40-something, very efficient lady who lives in the Midlands. What she does for a living I will keep from you for now. All will become clear later...

DW: Tell me when you have landed, Jennie.

J: I have landed. It's very black – I can't see anything at all.

DW: Put your hand out and tell me what you feel.

J: A hard wall, a brick wall, with bits sticking out. There are damp smells, things shuffling around... I can feel a hessian sack, sense some movement.

DW: Are you male or female?

J: Female, a teenager about 14. My name is Anne and it's 1753.

DW: How did you get where you are?

J: I'm on a dirty street in London. I am just standing there. I am about 12 years old now. I'm alone with no family – very alone. I think there is something wrong with my lung. I don't eat properly either, I feel as if I am just there, just exist.

It's daytime now, the streets are narrow and I am following a stream – no, it's a sewer that's running through them.

I can see a tunnel, a black dark place. It's where I was when I started.

DW: Why did you go that way?

J: I had to go into it. I was being forced to go in that direction. I have the instinct to hide away. I am supposed to be in the dark. I feel I become the dark if I go into the dark.

(Jennie then begins to go into things that are clearly from her childhood in this life. She is gently guided back to her past memories.)

DW: What is happening now?

J: I am coming out of a bend round a passage-way into the woods. I see a mound of wood twigs. It's a hut in the wood. It feels as if it's mine. It *is* mine and you get to it by going through the tunnel. There's a small bird's nest and what look like twigs and a shelf all the way round it – a shelf or is it a step? I'm not sure. I live off the forest, eat what I find. It's not much of a life. I feel abandoned.

(Suddenly it seems as if she just gives in.)

DW: Where do you find yourself now?

J: Starved to death. I was alone all my life. Damp, loneliness, dark...

DW: See the light, Jennie. Go into it and tell me when you are completely surrounded by it.

J: OK.

DW: Now what do you see?

J: It smells lovely. There are sounds – calming, peaceful.

DW: Go further into the light.

J: I can see a big house. A big house. A grey stone house...

(It becomes clear to me that Jennie has gone into another life. This sometimes happens and of course has to be followed through!)

DW: Where are you?

J: There's nothing on my feet, I am nine years old and I live in this house, used to – I feel attached. I'm playing in the nursery. Emily is my name. It's 1716. South something house – 'Ravenscourt Manor'.

It's bedtime and I am getting medicine for my chest. There is a nurse in a white cap. She looks like my mother in this life. I have one minute playing in bed. I don't see my parents often in that life. I see more of the nurse.

DW: Is there anyone else with you?

J: No. I can see someone playing there now. It's a boy, but he doesn't see me. I am in front of him and he doesn't see me.

(It becomes clear to me at this point that Emily is haunting her former home. She is visiting her family from the astral worlds, which would explain why she went from there into this life. I wait for her to confirm this. She soon realizes it.)

J: I am dead. I can see a grave on grass. Inside I feel so cold – feel cold. *[She means physically in the here and now.]* I can see a golden bright light. There's someone there. He's lifting his arm up. I'm going towards him, going to take his hand. It's Raphael. He is offering healing. I feel lifted, floating. It's not him who is making me feel that way – I just feel that way. I feel as if I am at sea, floating... Beautiful colours, amazing colours...

(Jennie begins to shake at this point, but as the archangel Raphael holds her she calms

down and starts to look more at peace. This is only the second time in all the regressions I have done that Raphael has done this.)

J: In the light I can see a nun's habit. I can't see her face, but I know she is a guide.

DW: What negatives do you want to leave behind from this life?

J: Being a little girl on my own.

DW: What positives can you bring back with you?

J: I loved the nurse. I think she is my mum now.

Now I can tell you what Jennie does: she is a regional manager and fundraiser for a charity working with children who are terminally ill, making their wishes come true. Could her past-life experiences have brought her into an incarnation where she helps children because of her soul's understanding of how it feels to be a child who is alone?

Her regression was interesting on many levels. First there was the link with what she does now and second there was the period spent haunting her own home – or was she just saying goodbye to it? Maybe she hadn't realized at that point that she had crossed. The presence of Raphael is also interesting; this isn't a common event and makes me wonder just what links further past-life regressions could uncover with him. Happily, Jennie wants to explore more and I look forward to it!

Here's what she had to say:

My PLR with David exceeded all my expectations. Opening my eyes to past lives made me feel whole and at peace in a very strange way, as though I was being put back in contact with something I had lost. It was extremely sad to remember those desperate lives, and although one life was full of privilege and the other beyond poverty and desperation, they had one thing in common and that was loneliness.

Remembering that in one of those lives I had something wrong with my lung, how's this for a coincidence: I had to be treated for TB as a very small child and my mum always said that I had one lung weaker than the other.

The one thing that has been a huge priority in my life is family and I have a fear of being alone. I think that this tiny glimpse into a couple of my past lives shows just why my family is so important to me now.

Afterwards, instead of feeling drained and needing tea and biscuits, I felt relieved, almost floating and buzzing with excitement!

Jennie is awaiting a date for another regression, hopefully to see another life where events will shed light on this incarnation and where she goes from here, using the fact that she has understood and released some negative traits to focus on the positive. I am sure she will visit a life that shows even more of the strengths I know are within this extraordinary woman.

CHAPTER 14

CATHY

And now, Cathy. Cathy has a soul that sung to me the moment we met. It was one of those instant things where you can see the hurt and the sadness below the bravado, see the beauty and serenity beyond the hectic personality...

She was introduced to me when I was having some work done in my house. She was to project-manage my new kitchen. When I first saw her I thought she was a very strong and very glamorous woman and as time went by I became friends with her, but she had a secret that coincidentally wasn't going to be a secret much longer. One day she was late to a meeting at my house and here's why: she had been hounded by the press all that day, as her ex-husband was on trial – for murder. It had been a very long time since Cathy had seen this man – they had been married when she was very young – but now her past had caught up with her and the press was doing what the press does – invading her privacy at any opportunity.

As things calmed down I asked Cathy if she would be interested in having some past-life work done. For me, it was fascinating to think she might have chosen to incarnate with this horrible man. If she had, what sort of things did they have to resolve and where did it come from? I also wanted to help Cathy, who at this point wasn't sure what was going to happen next. She was a successful woman who was getting on with things but, as you can imagine, having the past come back in such a way was taking its toll and she was seeing a counsellor.

Here's an account of the three regressions Cathy underwent, all at my house:

Cathy

Session One

DW: Can you tell me when you have landed, Cathy, and what you're wearing on your feet?

C: OK, I have landed. I'm not wearing anything on my feet and I am outdoors.

DW: Are you male or female?

C: Male.

(At this point Cathy starts to simply tell her tale. When clients do this it's often best to

*let them talk and not interfere at all. This is
what she had to say.)*

I have bad legs, not many clothes. My hair
is black. There's nobody with me at all. I'm
walking towards some trees, hunting for
food. I know I have a family and I am trying
to get some food to feed them.

There's a pig thing ahead of me. I grab it and
break its neck, take it back to the family camp,
where I see a fire. There's my family, my wife
and children, in the background. I don't recognize my wife from my current life but we
are in love. She has a baby on her back, a boy,
and there are another two children around,
two girls.

(She moves on about two months.)

We are a long way from camp, looking for
something – new space, I think. Everything
falls on my shoulders but I seem capable and
know just what to do.

We've found a new place, a good place. They
all appear from nowhere. Magic – it must be
magic.

(Later.)

I'm getting on a bit now. I see a big boat.
There's only me now, wading out to sea, just

me, and why I am getting in the boat I don't know. There seems to have been some trouble. I'm going to safety, but nowhere is safe any more. All the others are dead.

There are people with big knives. They don't like us much. They are invaders.

I'm getting into the boat.

Now I am on a beach. It looks familiar. Now it's normal to be on my own. My wife and family are dead – that's life! I can't expect any more.

(Cathy says this in a very matter-of-fact way. Could this be a tired old soul remembering past let-downs and simply saying that's how it goes? Is this her soul's experience, and if it is, will she have similar lives or will she let go of that cycle? She moves six months on.)

I am sitting on my own. I never meet anyone else, I'm always on my own...

(She cries at this point. Encouraged to let it all out, she cries some more, sobbing. When she's ready we carry on.)

He just sits down, gives up and dies. He's about 55 years old.

DW: Go into the light.

C: It's beautiful when he goes. It's so lovely, so beautiful, such light... There's nobody in the light to greet me from that life, but my mum is there from this life.

(Then eventually Cathy is surrounded by family – family from this life who have crossed, not from the past life. She doesn't say much, she seems distant and I leave her with her thoughts for a while.)

DW: What negative things do you want to leave behind from that life?

C: Isolation and not paying enough attention to others.

DW: What positive things would you like to bring forward to this life?

C: Love.

Cathy had a life where she was the support for everyone but she lost it when she couldn't do anything about the situation she found herself in. She had limits, like the rest of us.

The manner and delivery of her life suggest to me that Cathy has an old soul, one that gets through things life by life, seeing things pretty much the same as before, treating it all as a plod. So what does that tell her? It tells me she has slowed down a bit and may need to recognize that change comes from the individual, but the most important thing for *this* life I think Cathy could learn is that she's doing fine, she's one of life's survivors and needs to give herself a break! Part of her onward journey of easing up on herself will be accepting her own immense talents rather than judging herself for the occasional lapses that we all fall foul of now and again.

Her family from her previous life would have been in the light waiting to meet her, but she didn't see them – in effect she chose to ignore them. Could it be that she felt she failed them or is the truth simply that she couldn't face looking at them, knowing that if they forgave her the grief would be too much to bear?

We'll get Cathy's comments at the end of all three of the regressions we did together. Here's the second one:

Cathy

Session Two

DW: What are you wearing on your feet?

C: Nothing, I'm wearing nothing. I can't see, can't see anything at all.

(Cathy starts wringing her hands and carries on all the way through this regression.)

DW: Put your hand out. Can you feel anything?

C: I can feel stone walls, smooth walls, smooth and warm. I'm female, in my late twenties, and I am in prison. It doesn't feel that long ago – 1930, 1940, something like that.

DW: Why are you in prison?

C: I don't know. I don't see anyone. They make us walk on our own. I see nobody.

DW: Go back to a time before prison for me, Cathy. Where do you find yourself?

C: I'm on a street, walking. It looks like Prague, that sort of European city. I'm walking, my hair's a mess, I look dreadful, I am wearing crap, cheap, horrible clothes! *[Cathy is always immaculately presented in this life.]* I work as a vegetable grower, selling them at market.

DW: Do you know your name?

C: It's Karina, Karina Schultz. My hair is really messy! I have no husband, no children. I am at home now. It's a stone cottage with one room – that's it, one room. I am growing vegetables out of town. There's smoke coming out of my chimney. My parents are alive, very old and living somewhere else.

DW: Why were you in prison?

C: I did nothing wrong, I was just picked up off the street. I don't understand why. I just lived on my own and came into town to sell things. I think people saw that as odd. I expect it now, I expect it. The town is intolerant, but I don't complain.

Now I am being taken out of the prison – I have been shot!

Yes, that's about right – I was left a long time in the dark, then taken out and shot! The police shot me. I was a waste of space, but they couldn't do it legally, so they took me just outside the prison, opened a door and shot me.

(Cathy now goes into the light after her death.)

There are faces trying to get in, but they aren't able to. It's as if I am inside a balloon. I can see my granny from my current life. Burst the balloon – I am going to burst the balloon.

Now I am floating, floating around the sky. There is someone behind me – he's not a very nice person. He is angry at me, angry at me. He's my current husband, my second husband. He's angry because I left him behind, reincarnated without him... I hold him and he understands.

(At this point I am aware of Cathy's guide in the light and ask her to turn around and see if she can make him out.)

I can see the shadowy figure of a man. It feels as if he's like an animal, a horse, a powerful thing, supportive.

(I leave Cathy to talk to her guide.)

He says I am on my own because I am capable. Does that mean I always have to be on my own?

(Cathy is told she has chosen to be on her own.)

DW: What negative thing do you want to leave behind from that life?

C: Nothing.

DW: What positive attributes do you want to bring into this life?

C: Independence. Is that the same as being alone?

Again a solitary life, and one where she was also persecuted for being different, so it's interesting that Cathy said there was nothing she wanted to leave behind and then chose independence as her strength. Could it be that she is getting exactly what she wants from these lives? Is it a series of lives looking at isolation and independence? Or has she not noticed she is getting what she's asking for because she hasn't noticed she's asking for it? And what of her relationship with her ex-husband? Was this new karma created in her current incarnation or was he from further back than we have travelled?

There was one more regression to have and the next life was to be the most revealing:

Cathy

Session Three

Before Cathy arrived that day the atmosphere was very heavy and I had to ask for it to be lightened by my guides, as I wanted the energy to flow easily for Cathy.

DW: What are you wearing on your feet?

C: Sandals. They are like those Roman things with straps up the legs.

DW: Are you indoors or out?

C: Outdoors. I'm female, about 20 years old. I am wearing a tunic sort of thing, a dress. It's short – above the knee. I have long hair and it's loose and blonde.

DW: Can you describe the terrain?

C: It's rocky, hilly. It looks Scandinavian and as usual I am on my own.

DW: What are you doing there?

C: Looking at the hills, walking, just walking around looking for something – not sure what, but it has something to do with animals... It's goats! I am looking for my goats. I'm going to take them to market to sell. I hope to see them soon!

Now I am outside, camping *en route* and it's getting dark. I'm eating alone again. I have no family – no sense of ever having one.

DW: Go to the next day for me, Cathy. Where do you find yourself?

C: Animals are with me, my goats. They are just walking alongside me. I'm not worried about them straying. They are just following me.

I get the word 'Salzburg' [Austria]. There are cobbled streets, it's really busy and I can see lots of people – bakers, dressmakers. I feel as if I'm going to meet a man later.

I put the goats into an auction. The people there will sort it all out for me, so now I'm off to meet my man. He's very good looking, with thick black hair. He's wearing a white shirt and is tanned and has bright blue eyes. His name is Samuel and mine is Anita. He has my second husband's eyes. He's a black-smith. We are flirting – that's all it's been so far, just flirting, but we chat and he comes for a walk along the river with me. It's lovely.

After that we separate. I have to go and get the money for my goats.

DW: What happens now?

C: I am going to see an older couple. I stay with them. They are pleased to see me. I think I have known them since I was a child. They are in their fifties. I eat well that night.

My parents are off doing something, I'm not sure what, and I don't have any brothers or sisters.

Next day I am up early having a lovely break-fast, then I go to see Samuel. We're having a huge snog! I am going away for a couple of days, but I know I will see him again. I'm not sure how he feels about me, but he seems happy.

I walk home with my money and I am very happy. My house is small, functional, with one big room. It's open-plan and comfort-able but with very plain colours – basic. I'm not poor – comfortable, I would say. I am going to get more goats and breed and sell them. When I get some free time I read a lot and paint landscapes and happy things, for myself.

DW: Move to another time you find significant.

C: It's still warm, I've gone back to see my man and he is running towards me with his arms open, happy to see me. We are really in love. I don't want to let him go, though I have to get back to the goats. I've got to see the goats.

He lives above the forge. We get married. I am barefoot and pregnant, happy, and everything is very colourful.

(Cathy sees her life in brighter colours from this point. The greys disappear.)

We build a house near the goats and we have four children – two of each.

(Cathy cries at this point.)

I miss that joy, that simplicity. Everything is so hard and I am so bored with fighting for everything.

DW: When you're ready, tell me what you see.

C: She's dying. She's only about 40, but it's OK. Her children are around her. They seem to be teenagers, so they understand what's going on, and her husband is there. He can cope.

(She goes into the light.)

DW: Can you sense anyone in the light?

C: Just me. The light seems to be alive; it seems to be a moving thing.

DW: What negative thing do you want to leave behind from that life?

C: There isn't anything. Positive attributes – all of it!

Cathy had given her watercolour paints away that week – maybe she shouldn't have! Painting could help her remember the beauty of incarnating into a physical body rather than the grey days.

Cathy's first husband didn't put in an appearance in her past lives and given the high profile of the court case and the shadow he was casting over her life at the time it's a surprise, but the simple fact that he didn't provides proof that her lives were real experiences. If her subconscious had been making up images to deal with things that were happening at the time, he would definitely have appeared in some way, shape or form, as he was such a strong presence in her life at the time of the regressions. All day long she was being bombarded with requests for interviews about him, but in her past lives there was no sign of him. She may have come to an end of that cycle and have no need to know what role, if any, he played in her past lives, or she may have blocked it out because it's too difficult to deal with right now, or perhaps, and this is my front runner, she has a very powerful soul and has chosen to use past-life regression to kick herself up the backside, remind herself that actually life doesn't have to be a struggle and when you find someone you can rely on you can build a better life and go from black and white to colour.

Cathy herself commented:

I wasn't sure what to expect from past-life regression and given my past in this life, I was a little apprehensive, but David's reassurance and gentle manner put me at ease.

The theme of the lives seems to have been loneliness, but I have seen that as a strength and whilst I have always sought the company of others in this life and never really been on my own, always being surrounded by flatmates, house mates or partners, now I feel that if I were to be on my own it wouldn't be an issue. I could cope, and I think I could cope well, which in an odd way has made having a relationship easier!

As David says, my ex-husband didn't make an appearance in any of my regressions. I thought about that and I feel I was with him in the past but this time I was strong enough to get away from him and my intuition tells me that if I ever meet him again in future lives I will say no to him immediately, no matter what the circumstances. David has suggested that we spin away from people as karma is resolved and I feel that may very well be the case.

Now I find myself in a situation where I am starting again and this time I am thinking of my personal creativity, how I can bring the colour back into my life and make it a life well lived. My regressions were sad in places and my life in this incarnation has been too, but now things are getting brighter and I am looking forwards – all thanks to the past in an odd sort of way!

Thank you, David.

CHAPTER 15

PAST-LIFE ASTROLOGY

We all have our own reasons for incarnating, but what are they? Earlier I mentioned that astrology can offer you the chance to discover more about them. In fact, your whole birth chart can be interpreted as a past-life experience. That's sort of what it is – a look at what you have done and where you have chosen to make some changes in this incarnation – but time and space dictate that we can only look at a little at a time. In my first two books we looked at the sun sign and the nodes of the moon, both south and north. This time it's the turn of Saturn.

Saturn

Saturn is sometimes seen as the karma planet and I guess in some ways he is, but he generally indicates where you're likely to find responsibility. He reminds you of where you have committed to make amends and where perhaps you have decided to take on some extra work to get extra points in the game of life. He also reminds you of what you can do very well, even if it has been born from incarnations where you have struggled. His influence will be tempered by the way he interacts with the other planets and the house or section of the chart he finds himself in, so the interpretations given here are only a starting point. As ever, the best way to find out more is to seek the help of a qualified astrologer or learn more yourself!

My own Saturn is in Capricorn in the third house, which in brief means I have accepted the role of communicator, and a very serious one at that, but thankfully the humour of Capricorn gives me a break now and again. Where is he for you? Check out the list at the back of the book to locate where he was when you were born, then read on to find out what this means for you.

SATURN IN ARIES

This suggests you may have had lives as a self-starter, highly motivated and full of your own self-worth, but sometimes you may have rushed ahead and that blundering could have led you to want to make amends for mistakes, albeit made with the best of intentions! Often you have to fight for what you want in life, but all is possible, as your determination easily outshines that of others. You're likely to find it easy to put yourself in charge, but the lesson may be about control and learning to act with more diplomacy and in a fairer way with those you have to live and work with. Past lives as leaders, sometimes military, are shown by Saturn in Aries.

SATURN IN TAURUS

A desire to be secure and to have material possessions is top of your list, getting your house in order, 'feeling sorted' in the modern vernacular, but beware, this can make you a little reluctant to part with the cash when letting it flow may be a better way of dealing with things. You are practical and highly principled, but don't take success for granted. A young woman I know of with this placement recently won a large amount on the lottery. With that comes great responsibility and although she will be able to deal with it, it may not be the most comfortable of things for a while. If you have this placement, don't take security for granted – the test is whether you can keep it! Past lives of financial authority and power are shown by Saturn in Taurus.

SATURN IN GEMINI

This makes a person very disciplined in making choices, but their emotive and intuitive side may suffer as a consequence. Bring a little balance to the equation, or the intellect could rush into cunning ideas that have little space for the feelings of others, and that's something you don't want to encourage! Working in communications is a great way to express this Saturn placement. That will give an outlet for that cool, calm, collected factual delivery. You may find your thoughts running away with you on occasions. That's the Gemini part of the equation. Let it happen, as it's part of your creative process, and pretty soon you will reel those thoughts back in and restore genius throughout the land. Past lives where you have had to think on your feet are indicated by this placement.

SATURN IN CANCER

This shows you have committed to take care of the family, and sometimes it may seem as if you put them before your own wellbeing. There's nothing wrong with that, of course, but sometimes they would be more than capable of sorting out their own stuff if only you would step back. Family karma can be heightened with Saturn here and you may have chosen situations where relationships between you and your parents or children are strained, the idea being you learn more that way and knowing when to step forward and when to step back will eventually sort it all out! This placement could also indicate a need for tradition and rules, and what better place to learn those than in a family?!

SATURN IN LEO

Do you feel the need for recognition, to be seen and heard and the ruler of all you survey? And just where is your crown? Did you bring it with you when you incarnated? Maybe you don't want to be in the public eye this time, but finding the balance between stepping out and being seen as the leader you are and retreating is crucial if you have this placement. You will have to feed your need for an audience, but on the other hand nurture those close to you in order to feel your court surrounding you. A client of mine with this placement is a very talented actress and even though she works hard and is good at what she does, she is never happier than when she's with her kids just playing around – that is, until she misses the applause! Saturn in Leo shows past lives in the public eye and the ability to handle that again.

SATURN IN VIRGO

Grab your list, you might want to write this down! You'll have a tendency towards pickiness, systems and the right way to do things, as this is where Saturn puts on his anorak and gets a hobby. You're likely to be very successful at detailed work and will have the ability to get the job done like nobody else can, but make sure that in your drive to get it done properly you don't fail to see that sometimes rules can be bent a little when the need arises. Your ability to spot things that others don't is the real blessing you've brought from your past lives, and even though that can be a nightmare for those who live with you, your intentions are usually good ones! Past lives where you have had to rely on your ability to see what others miss are shown by your choice of Saturn in Virgo.

SATURN IN LIBRA

You may not want to commit to someone – in fact, you could fight it for a long time – but once you do, nothing is going to make you budge, as Saturn is in the sign of relationships when he's sitting exalted in Libra. You're a great organizer on a group level and able to balance the energies of those who might not naturally mix – you're the salt in the salad dressing making the oil and water into an emulsion! Getting mixed up with the law is highly possible too. Thankfully you're more likely to be sorting things out than being on the other side! With this placement you're likely to have had past lives where you were a counsellor, a lawyer finding the balance and keeping it.

SATURN IN SCORPIO

A sense of keen business awareness is the strength brought about by this placement and knowing your business partners inside out is often a given. As with all the Saturn placements, it's how positively the planet is aspected that shows whether the strengths or weaknesses are prevalent. The weakness of this one, however, is worth mentioning, as it can affect you in an intensely emotional way, making some things seem worse than they are or causing you to dwell on things far too much and to seek respite through materialism and self-indulgence. Finding a role in life where you can be passionate about what you do for a living often helps – channel your energy towards success! Previous lives as solitary spiritual seekers or decadent and hedonistic individuals are common – from one extreme to the other!

SATURN IN SAGITTARIUS

With Saturn here the focus is on learning, travel and embracing the cultures of others through reading or getting out into the big wide world. A search for who you are and what you actually believe in and having it proven back to you is prevalent and many born with this placement are outspoken about what they consider to be right and wrong. The lesson may be to realize that each one of us has our own road to travel and whilst debate is a good thing, preaching may not be! However, there's a natural temperance to this placement; it's one that says you have great knowledge and if you use it with the flow adjuster that Saturn can be, it should produce results: someone who knows what's right, what's right now and who it's right to tell about it. In past lives you may have been royal, with your word being law. Learning that it's a democracy now may be a lesson – or three!

SATURN IN CAPRICORN

This is Saturn's home, so he is very happy here and he shows his natural ability to lead and to get things right! If you have Saturn here, you are someone who can plan a career path very well and rarely, if ever, makes mistakes along the way, taking on new projects only when all the homework is done. The downside may be a tendency to assume that everyone is as efficient as you and it comes as a bit of a disappointment when they aren't! Seeing an opportunity to get ahead comes from a previous lifetime, a time when you may not have been in the seat of power but the one making it all happen. Past lives where you were given a lot of responsibility have prepared you for this incarnation where you actively seek it.

SATURN IN AQUARIUS

Setting yourself free is something that's important for you – free from restrictions of class or creed, free to do what you want when you want. This is the lesson of Saturn in Aquarius. You can be brighter than a bright thing, but is your genius that of Sherlock Holmes or Doctor Moriarty?! Knowing your own mind is something you're likely to spend a lot of time on and any discipline that works through the mind works very well for you – NLP, for example. You're human and will always stand up for the underdog – in fact you're likely to relish that particular challenge, as regard for authority isn't exactly high on your list. You may be here to improve your intellectual standing, so study and experience as much as you can. Past lives as artists, poets, free thinkers and the leaders of such people are likely.

SATURN IN PISCES

This is a tough placement, as Saturn in the sign where imagination runs wild and the world of memories can rule over a more practical approach is not a natural mix, but if used wisely, your ability to create pictures nobody else can see can be profitable as well as cathartic! This is the placement of the photographer, the film maker, the fantasy writer, the people whose magical worlds can intrigue and entertain us all. Working with those less fortunate than yourself can also be a reminder of the struggle some go through on Earth and of just how fortunate your own incarnation may be, for you will be allowed time to dream. In past lives a retreat into the world of the imagination may have been your only respite in tough times, but now it's about bringing your inner world out and astounding everyone with your deep and meaningful insights.

CHAPTER 16

OVER TO YOU...

So you've learned – I hope – a lot about past lives and along the way there have been some meditations and ways for you to take a closer look at your own journey. We have established you will make up your own mind about what you think and how you will go about finding out more, but how about some ideas from the modern world to shake it all up? Could you have a 'Come as your past life' party? For those who don't know what their past lives have been, no worries, just let their subconscious direct them to the right costume...! Light-hearted fun, I know, but imagine the conversations, and could the simple act of dressing up bring it all back?

What about having a group regression with some friends? Use the Akashic records meditation (*see pages 67–70*) and compare notes. See whether you feel their lives as well as your own. Have you shared some incarnations? Maybe you have been friends for centuries?

What about combining astrology with your past-life experiences and seeing what you come up with? Or, if you read tarot cards, think about your past-life memories and then take up your cards, effectively reading for your past-life self!

The only limits to what you can do are set by your own imagination and it's been my experience that our imagination sets no limits!

It's about learning more from your soul and that information that will spur your personality on to greater things and maybe help you leave what's not for you behind you with grace and acceptance.

I know the impact that past-life work can have. I still see some of the people in this book on a weekly or monthly basis and they have all changed as a consequence of their experiences, changed in many ways, but the one common thing is that they have gained the understanding that nothing is forever and have had the courage to make life happen rather than let life happen to them.

Ultimately, you will make up your own mind about past-life regression, but I hope you will make it up after experiencing one. There's a list at the back of the book to help you find someone near you. These are people who have contributed to the book in some way, but I haven't been to see them personally. So remember the rules: take someone with you, feel comfortable and keep asking those questions!

It has been a pleasure not only doing the regressions for this book but also reading and listening to all of the many hundreds of stories sent to me. Unfortunately I couldn't include them all, but if you sent me one, thank you so much.

As you move forward with your own journey, look to your past for answers that will make the here and now easier for you. Life's not meant to be a struggle and those who look for answers will find them.

Blessed Be
David

LOCATING SATURN

1900 Jan.21 08:10 Cap	1926 Dec.02 22:36 Sag	1956 May 14 03:40 Sco	1985 Nov.17 02:13 Sag
1900 Jul.18 17:35 Sag	1929 Mar.15 15:34 Cap	1956 Oct.10 15:14 Sag	1988 Feb.13 23:55 Cap
1900 Oct.17 05:04 Cap	1929 May 05 04:07 Sag	1959 Jan.05 13:36 Cap	1988 Jun.10 05:13 Sag
1903 Jan.19 22:17 Aqu	1929 Nov.30 04:24 Cap	1962 Jan.03 19:05 Aqu	1988 Nov.12 09:31 Cap
1905 Apr.13 08:39 Pis	1932 Feb.24 02:50 Aqu	1964 Mar.24 04:22 Pis	1991 Feb.06 18:56 Aqu
1905 Aug.17 00:40 Aqu	1932 Aug.13 11:13 Cap	1964 Sep.16 20:57 Aqu	1993 May 21 05:17 Pis
1906 Jan.08 12:50 Pis	1932 Nov.20 02:14 Aqu	1964 Dec.16 05:46 Pis	1993 Jun.30 07:53 Aqu
1908 Mar.19 14:25 Ari	1935 Feb.14 14:11 Pis	1967 Mar.03 21:36 Ari	1994 Jan.28 23:48 Pis
1910 May 17 07:30 Tau	1937 Apr.25 06:32 Ari	1969 Apr.29 22:26 Tau	1996 Apr.07 08:54 Ari
1910 Dec.14 23:08 Ari	1937 Oct.18 03:40 Pis	1971 Jun.18 16:11 Gem	1998 Jun.09 06:13 Tau
1911 Jan.20 09:26 Tau	1938 Jan.14 10:34 Ari	1972 Jan.10 03:42 Tau	1998 Oct.25 18:32 Ari
1912 Jul.07 06:14 Gem	1939 Jul.06 05:49 Tau	1972 Feb.21 15:02 Gem	1999 Mar.01 01:33 Tau
1912 Nov.30 18:18 Tau	1939 Sep.22 05:10 Ari	1973 Aug.01 22:23 Can	2000 Aug.10 02:38 Gem
1913 Mar.26 13:08 Gem	1940 Mar.20 09:43 Tau	1974 Jan.07 20:23 Gem	2000 Oct.16 00:33 Tau
1914 Aug.24 17:29 Can	1942 May 08 19:41 Gem	1974 Apr.18 22:38 Can	2001 Apr.20 22:00 Gem
1914 Dec.07 06:45 Gem	1944 Jun.20 07:50 Can	1975 Sep.17 05:00 Leo	2003 Jun.04 01:28 Can
1915 May 11 21:24 Can	1946 Aug.02 14:44 Leo	1976 Jan.14 13:10 Can	2005 Jul.16 12:31 Leo
1916 Oct.17 15:37 Leo	1948 Sep.19 04:38 Vir	1976 Jun.05 05:12 Leo	2007 Sep.02 13:49 Vir
1916 Dec.07 19:12 Can	1949 Apr.03 03:40 Leo	1977 Nov.17 02:51 Vir	2009 Oct.29 17:09 Lib
1917 Jun.24 13:54 Leo	1949 May 29 13:04 Vir	1978 Jan.05 00:35 Leo	2010 Apr.07 18:55 Vir
1919 Aug.12 13:53 Vir	1950 Nov.20 15:53 Lib	1978 Jul.26 12:06 Vir	2010 Jul.21 15:09 Lib
1921 Oct.07 17:22 Lib	1951 Mar.07 12:07 Vir	1980 Sep.21 10:52 Lib	2012 Oct.05 20:34 Sco
1923 Dec.20 04:27 Sco	1951 Aug.13 16:47 Lib	1982 Nov.29 10:33 Sco	
1924 Apr.06 08:32 Lib	1953 Oct.22 15:38 Sco	1983 May 06 19:24 Lib	
1924 Sep.13 22:01 Sco	1956 Jan.12 18:49 Sag	1983 Aug.24 12:00 Sco	

RESOURCES

Deborah Monshin
www.soul-healing.org.uk

Alice Potter
Key2change Hypnotherapy
www.key2change.co.uk

Jeff Powell
Past Life Therapies
www.pastlifetherapies.com

Jenny Smedley
www.jennysmedley.com

Notes

Notes

Notes

We hope you enjoyed this Hay House book.
If you would like to receive a free catalogue featuring additional
Hay House books and products, or if you would like information
about the Hay Foundation, please contact:

Hay House UK Ltd
292B Kensal Rd • London W10 5BE
Tel: (44) 20 8962 1230; Fax: (44) 20 8962 1239
www.hayhouse.co.uk

***

Published and distributed in the United States of America by:
Hay House, Inc. • PO Box 5100 • Carlsbad, CA 92018-5100
Tel.: (1) 760 431 7695 or (1) 800 654 5126;
Fax: (1) 760 431 6948 or (1) 800 650 5115
www.hayhouse.com

Published and distributed in Australia by:
Hay House Australia Ltd • 18/36 Ralph St • Alexandria NSW 2015
Tel.: (61) 2 9669 4299; Fax: (61) 2 9669 4144
www.hayhouse.com.au

Published and distributed in the Republic of South Africa by:
Hay House SA (Pty) Ltd • PO Box 990 • Witkoppen 2068
Tel./Fax: (27) 11 467 8904 • www.hayhouse.co.za

Published and distributed in India by:
Hay House Publishers India • Muskaan Complex • Plot No.3
B-2 • Vasant Kunj • New Delhi – 110 070.
Tel.: (91) 11 41761620; Fax: (91) 11 41761630.
www.hayhouse.co.in

Distributed in Canada by:
Raincoast • 9050 Shaughnessy St • Vancouver, BC V6P 6E5
Tel.: (1) 604 323 7100; Fax: (1) 604 323 2600

***

Sign up via the Hay House UK website to receive the Hay House
online newsletter and stay informed about what's going on with
your favourite authors. You'll receive bimonthly announcements
about discounts and offers, special events, product highlights,
free excerpts, giveaways, and more!
www.hayhouse.co.uk